COMMON PRAYER ON
COMMON GROUND

COMMON PRAYER ON COMMON GROUND

A Vision of Anglican Orthodoxy

ALAN JONES

MOREHOUSE PUBLISHING

HARRISBURG · PENNSYLVANIA

Unless otherwise noted, the Scripture quotations contained herein are from
the New Revised Standard Version Bible, copyright © 1989 by the Division
of Christian Education of the National Council of Churches of Christ in
the U.S.A. Used by permission. All rights reserved.

"At the Smithville Methodist Church." Copyright © 1986 by Stephen Dunn,
from New and Selected Poems 1974–1994 by Stephen Dunn.
Used by permission of W. W. Norton and Company, Inc.

Morehouse Publishing, P.O. Box 1321, Harrisburg, PA 17105

Morehouse Publishing, 445 Fifth Avenue, New York, NY 10016

Morehouse Publishing is an imprint of Church Publishing Incorporated.

Cover art: Laurie Klein Westhafer

Cover design: Laurie Klein Westhafer

Library of Congress Cataloging-in-Publication Data

Jones, Alan W., 1940-
   Common prayer on common ground : a vision of
Anglican orthodoxy / Alan Jones.
      p. cm.
   Includes bibliographical references and index.
   ISBN-13: 978-0-8192-2247-3 (pbk.)
   1. Anglican Communion—Doctrines. I. Title.
BX5005.J66 2006
283—dc22
                                    2006004859

Printed in the United States of America

06 07 08 09   10 9 8 7 6 5 4 3 2 1

DEDICATION

In thanksgiving for the witness of six archbishops,
exemplars of Anglican Orthodoxy

Michael Ramsey

Robert Runcie

Rowan Williams

Desmond Tutu

Frank Griswold

Peter Carnley

CONTENTS

PREFACE

*O God of truth and peace, you raised up your servant Richard Hooker in
a day of bitter controversy to defend with sound reasoning and great
charity the catholic and reformed religion: Grant that we may maintain
that middle way, not as a compromise for the sake of peace, but as a
comprehension for the sake of truth; through Jesus Christ our Lord, who
lives and reigns with you and the Holy Spirit, one God, for ever and ever.
Amen.*
—Collect, the Feast of Richard Hooker

*This may be counted among the greatest evils with which this
age is infected, that they which are called Christians are
miserably divided about Christ.*
—An Elizabethan lament

I wrote this book as the result of several sleepless nights over what was happening to the Anglican Communion. It became, in the end, a sort of love letter to Anglicanism. I was born into it and it's the one tradition that still
enables me to call myself a Christian. My hope is that this book will contribute
to a sane and grateful conversation about the genius of the Anglican Way and
its unique contribution to the ongoing and sadly often now ungracious and
bitter conversation going on worldwide about Christianity and its future.

> —Alan Jones
> Dean of Grace Cathedral, San Francisco,
> and Canon of the Cathedral of Our Lady of Chartres,
> The Feast of St. Michael and All Angels, 2005

ix

INTRODUCTON

Don't worry, my dear. We're just moving through an age of transition.
—Adam to Eve as they left the garden of Eden

In every soul there is an abyss of mystery . . . When these hidden things shall have been revealed to us, according to the Promise, there will be unimaginable surprises.
—Leon Bloy

The Sky is Falling!

There are people in every age who think the world is coming to an end. Novels record the crumbling of old worlds and the building of new ones. Consider, for example, Joseph Roth's *The Radetzky March*, about the falling apart of the Austro-Hungarian Empire; or Giuseppe di Lampedusa's *The Leopard*, about the disintegration and birth of what was to be Italy; or Paul Scott's *The Raj Quartet*, about the last gasp of the British rule of India. There are countless examples of epic stories of death and rebirth, and all of them, it seems, are filled with a mixture of expectation and regret: "It was the worst of times, it was the best of times." Or is it the other way round? When times are bad, we go shopping for solutions and ally ourselves to those on the left or right who offer them, because even the best of us can't bear the messiness of human history. The worst of us tend to be punitive. We want the human race to shape up or else. We want solutions. And when we go shopping for them, we often call it "getting back to basics."

In the church, too, there are those who think the end of the world is in sight. Certain that the world is going through some new Dark Ages, they've taken up a defensive and aggressive posture toward what they think are the basics. It's understandable. My liberal friends like to believe the church—with its stand on inclusion and its radical vision of hospitality—is becoming more prophetic. With regard to the present crisis in Anglicanism, some liberals think that the marginalization of American and Canadian Anglicans is a sign that the church is on the right track. We must be doing something right, they reason, if the rest of the world is against us.

My conservative friends think otherwise. They have their own set of "basics." The church, they are convinced, has lost its way and the liberals mistake pathology for prophecy. Both sides need to repent.

Back to Basics

This is nothing new. I remember, in the '60s in England, a group of so-called radicals wrote a book called *Soundings* and a more conservative group responded with a booklet entitled *Four Anchors from the Stern*. The controversy then was all very polite and looked very tame. But now the tone is bitter and mean-spirited. Each side tends to demonize the other, and the only thing they seem to agree about is that the Dark Ages are right around the corner. Although both sides see the bankruptcy of the secular project, one side wants to hold the line while the other is eager to usher in a brave new world.

Somewhere in the middle, though, there are those of us who, like me, simply don't know all the answers to the myriad problems facing us. We are not, however, without a compass. We have our list of basics too. Prayer and worship are central to us, and our hesitancy about quick answers to difficult issues has more to do with reverence for mystery than with absence of conviction.

It cannot be overemphasized that worship and communion are central to Anglican self-understanding. The liturgy prepares us for the liturgy ("service") in the world. We believe it connects us with life in heaven—a foretaste of what the world is called to be. We also believe that Scripture is to be interpreted from *within* the liturgy. Since worship pushes us into adoration and silence beyond words and definitions, Anglicanism is often misunderstood, even by those who love and admire the tradition, as something that "is hopelessly indefinite and conflicted"—a sort of do-it-yourself religion.[1] I don't think this is true but George Sumner, principal of Wycliffe College, Toronto, poses the right question: "Today what is at issue is, quite simply, the catholicity of Anglicanism. Are we to be part of the church catholic, or are we to devolve in North America, to two more sects, only with vestments?"[2] If I were forced to choose between following bishop X who is considered a "heretic" or bishop Y who is a schismatic, I would choose the former. I would rather protect catholicity than be an advocate of a local cause. I don't mean to imply that this would be an easy choice lightly taken because issues of truth and justice inevitably are central. Communion is the highest value for me not because questions of truth aren't central but because they are often elusive. History teaches us that truth is unnervingly elusive even as we are bound to pursue it. As Father Herbert Kelly, the founder of the Society of the Sacred Mission, used to say, "Only God is Catholic. The Catholic Church hasn't happened yet!"[3]

Ian T. Douglas of the Episcopal Divinity School, commenting on the Windsor Report, affirms that "communion is first and foremost about relationship and mission, not about structure and instruments."[4] So for us, schism is a greater sin than heresy: a view that is maddening to people who want to live in a tidier world. Some see this as "a matter of truth versus unity"—better to salvage a true church from the break-up than maintain a united one that has lost its way. Yet a united church that struggles with the fact of its brokenness can also be a powerful sign of Christ's truth, beyond what pristine ideological purity, be it liberal or conservative, can demonstrate."[5] I have great sympathy with those who say, "pursue integrity and unity will follow," but in practice this leads to more and more fragmentation. It's not a matter of compromising our integrity. It's a matter of our admitting that we don't know the answer to every question.

We don't know the answer, for example, to "gay marriage." We are clear and enthusiastic supporters of gay rights and of faithful gay relationships, but we struggle with the fact that the word "marriage" means several things. On the one hand, it means a civil contract with all the protections given by the state. If that's it, I'm for it. But the word has another meaning. Some of us believe that the word "marriage" might best be preserved to describe the celebration of the complementarity of the sexes and the privilege, when possible, of having children. Surely, with our genius for language, we can come up with something fresh to describe the new situation? (I've come to wish that the church would get out of the marriage business altogether. Let the state take care of it, then allow couples to go to the church, synagogue, or temple of their choice for the blessing of their tradition.)

Often the opponents *and* proponents of "gay marriage" come up with the same argument to support different conclusions. Bob Pitko, the bartender at the Ramrod Leather Denim Cruise Bar in Boston, believes that "the majority of gays will never get married. We want to have sex as much as we possibly can." One side points to a comment like this and says, "See how promiscuous 'they' are!" The other side believes that "marriage" will support the desire for stability and faithfulness in gay relationships. I hope so. Both statements are not only insulting but inaccurate—they could be as easily applied to heterosexuals. There seem to be plenty of those who want to have sex as often as possible, and a fair number for whom marriage would provide a measure of stability. Some of my liberal friends scoff at my hesitancy, and my conservative friends think that I went "soft" years ago because I am always looking for agreement where there is none.

Building Bridges

It's easy for me to find agreements because I've got an Anglican penchant for building bridges, and when I study the Anglican tradition I find myself very much at home in it and I am confident about its future. The best, I feel sure, is yet to come. I think the peculiar vocation of Anglicanism is to anticipate the future by being a bridge church. I know that's an old cliché but, at the risk of being misunderstood as advocating Anglican imperialism, in my lifetime I've seen Roman Catholicism and Protestantism become more and more "Anglican." The joke, of course, is on us, because this trend is never acknowledged. Roman Catholicism is much more open than it used to be, and there are signs that Protestants appreciate liturgy and tradition more and more. At the end of a series of lectures some years ago at the University of Dallas, an institution under the Dominican order, I announced, tongue-in-cheek, "The glory of Anglicanism is that in the end everyone will be Anglican. Its tragedy is that no one will know!"

It's an outrageous claim, of course, but there's a kernel of truth in it. It expresses both the strength and weakness of Anglicanism. There's an ancient phrase: *anima naturaliter Christiana*—the naturally Christian soul. It meant that if the soul were true to itself by freely responding to grace it would be Christian or, better, Christlike. One of my old teachers spoke of the *anima naturaliter Anglicana*—the naturally Anglican soul. The weakness and strength of being an Anglican, he pointed out, was that it was the most natural and spontaneous thing in the world, the most gracious way of being human. Arrogant? Naive? Yes, but it points to Anglicanism's basic humanism, and even its humility in being willing simply to disappear in God's good time. What sometimes infuriates non-Anglican Christians (and, to be honest, a new breed of Anglicans) is that traditional Anglicans don't see much of a distinction between Christians and non-Christians because they see many Christlike non-Christians and many un-Christlike Christians. Our take on religion is very practical and we believe that we have more in common with other human beings than anything that could possibly divide us.

As Anglicans, we are united by a vision of Christian humanism. We agree with one Roman Catholic commentator that the drama of the "Church's interaction with the modern world can be described as a dialogue, and at times a confrontation, between two new versions of humanism. One takes complete human autonomy as the ultimate good, and the other promotes a Christ-centered vision of human wholeness—human growth and development towards a model of perfection that is not humanity's own invention."[6] My quarrel with "liberalism" is that it tends to promote the doctrine of the autonomous self—a self separate from others, ultimately alone, and not responsible to other selves. The Anglican conviction, as far as I understand it, is that there is an intrinsic human orientation toward God. Separated from God, we make no sense—we are unintelligible. Moreover, we believe that there is a drive toward universality because there is but one human race.[7]

The Middle Way

What of my own practice—my own "basics"? The Eucharist is central to my spiritual life, and so is the Daily Office. I light candles before icons and invoke the protection of the holy angels. I feel distress at the "liberal" church, with its loss of transcendence and its ignorance of and lack of respect for tradition. I appreciate being able to say mass on Thursdays at the one *fixed* altar at the cathedral where I work and worship. In other words, I think of myself as a fairly conservative Anglican in the Catholic tradition. Others, no doubt, would place me somewhere else!

A friend of mine translates the famous opening of the Fourth Gospel: "In the beginning was the conversation. . . ." It is in conversation with God and with each other that we become truly alive. I suspect there are many out there like me—both Catholics and Evangelicals—who are rooted in the *via media* (the middle way) of Anglicanism but who feel that the great conversation (which is a way of describing the life of the church) at the heart of our faith has not only been abandoned but even rejected as a fundamental weakness. The extremes—on the one hand, those who embrace "inclusion" with no sense of reasonable discernment and, on the other, the punitive conservatives whose hard theology masks a mean spirit—have taken over. Both sides are impatient with conversation. "Why bother?" they demand. "What is there to talk about? We're right. We know the truth." This book is addressed to those in the middle who feel they have not much of a voice in the present raucous debate and are longing to revive the conversation.

And the conversation is critical. When we abandon talking to one another, joy goes out the window. In our panic and anxiety we lose an essential element of the gospel—joy and generosity of spirit—and find instead a prevailing sadness. Playwright David Hare, author of *Racing Demon*, a play about the Church of England, writes, "Many of the clergy I've met have pervasive melancholy—a sadness. You see it in their clothes. In their personal relationships."[8] If we're not careful, that pervasive melancholy will infect the whole church, a particular concern because the classic mark of the Christian is joy.

Welcome to the Banquet

In this spirit of love and joy, the true Christian mentality is more of a banquet than a fortress. But many of us have left the table and retreated into a fortress. These two attitudes to religion are evident in all the great religious traditions, leaving onlookers to wonder if we're protectors of a tradition or pilgrims into it? The fundamental question, "What kind of reality—banquet or fortress—do we live in?" underlies all our contentious wrangling.

Here's an example of that tension: Think of the two Roman Catholicisms represented by the response to Vatican II's Pastoral Constitution on the Church in the Modern World, *Gaudium et Spes*, which is as relevant today as it was forty years ago. There is, according to the English Roman Catholic weekly *The Tablet*, a growing temptation "to reduce Catholicism to a series of pat answers and correct rituals, conformity with which is demanded as a price for membership." Some seek to disparage the document "by describing it as dated, impossibly optimistic, fashionably liberal, pelagian and nothing more than the Council's unthinking afterthought."[9]

In the United States, the two Catholicisms are exemplified by the late Cardinal Joseph Bernardin of Chicago and the disgraced Cardinal Bernard Law, formerly of Boston. Not long before he died, Bernardin launched The Catholic Common Ground Project, calling for "a renewed spirit of civility, dialogue, generosity and broad serious consultation"—even with Catholic dissenters. Law's response: "The church already has Common Ground. . . . The crisis the church is facing can only be adequately addressed by a clarion call to conversion." But what kind of conversion? What Cardinal Law had in mind, it seems, was conversion to the absolute truth as he saw it. James Carroll, writing in the *Boston Globe*, commented, "The divide that really matters now is the one that separates believers, and that conflict is caught precisely by two different attitudes toward the 'absolute', which both parties affirm."[10] These two attitudes are alive and well in the Anglican Communion, too. The only thing those on opposite sides seem to have in common is their unwillingness to negotiate. Each side believes it is right and has nothing to learn from the other.

Sadly, we can trace these two mind-sets back through history. Consider the Council of Trent and the Second Vatican Council.

> At the conclusion of the Council of Trent in 1563, Pope Pius IV issued a papal Bull which is still echoing in our heads. It forbade, under pain of excommunication, any attempt by anyone at all "to publish, in any form, any commentaries, glosses, annotations, scholia, or any kind of interpretation whatsoever of the decrees of the said council." Even to explain why Trent was right, was wrong. This spirit of non-negotiability—of the final word having been finally spoken—became the central driving force of the Counter-Reformation. The Bull was calculated to stifle any further intellectual reflection or any possibility of evolution. The Catholic Church was henceforth to stay the way it was, for ever and ever, Amen.[11]

This spirit has now infected Anglicanism in a serious way. Rome has yet to recover and this is why the ARCIC—The Anglican–Roman Catholic International Commission—joint statement, *The Gift of Authority*, is a significant and welcome contribution to the conversation within the church about our future together.

Exactly four hundred years after the Council of Trent, Pope John XXIII, at the Second Vatican Council, did much to dispel the influence of Pius IV and the damage done by that earlier council. But that old attitude hasn't disappeared completely. Many Roman Catholics wish Vatican II had never happened. And many Anglicans wish the Prayer Book had never been revised, that women had never been ordained, and that gays had never been tolerated, let alone accepted. Anglicans, therefore, have no grounds to feel superior to their Roman Catholic cousins. The idea that faith is immutable and eternal instead of historically and culturally conditioned is very attractive to those who can't stand the contingencies of history.

Leon Bloy, 1846–1917, a French Roman Catholic and social reformer, wrote: "An obedient son of the Church, I am nonetheless in a communion of impatience with all the mutinous, all the disillusioned, all those who have cried and not been heard, all the damned of the world. . . !" This rebellious sentiment can be found in Anglicanism at its best. I like to think of Cardinal Bernardin and even John XXIII as closet Anglicans! As fanciful as this is, the idea of radical inclusion gives content to the vision of a joyful, fearless, and generous Christianity, which typifies Anglicanism at its best.

An Anglican Vision

This book is about my vision for living out this vibrant Christianity within the Anglican tradition. It is presented in four parts. In Part I, I'll look at the present climate that pits fundamentalism against "modernism" and examine the ways each impacts the crisis in Anglicanism today. Both extremes display an excessive "rationalism" that's entirely foreign to Anglicanism.

In Part II, I'll take a look at the caricatures of Anglicanism as a manifestation of muddled and fuzzy thinking.

In Part III, I'll define Anglican Orthodoxy (see its nine marks below). It can be a dangerous word meaning "right belief," but I think it's worth rehabilitating—as an orientation toward a transcendent mystery, seen, in part, through the eyes of two archbishops: Peter Carnley, the recently retired primate of Australia who has served on and been co-chair of the Anglican–Roman Catholic International Commission, and Rowan Williams, the archbishop of Canterbury—the best exponent of Catholic Anglicanism since Michael Ramsey. I am attracted to Rowan Williams not only because of his articulation of theology as a converting conversation with mystery but also because he is deaf in one ear. He has to listen carefully. Peter Cornwell comments:

> The archbishop is not at ease with shouted certainties. There is always in his theology a stammer, not because he is in doubt whether there is anything there but because he knows there is too much. Theology for him is always an encounter 'with what cannot be mastered'. Christians

have to stay together patiently in love, resisting the urge to parade convictions and go off to do their own thing with the likeminded. Instead
they should listen to one another.[12]

Finally, Part IV examines Anglicanism through the eyes of some of its
greatest exemplars, with special reference to John Donne and the struggles of
the seventeenth century.

There should be something here to offend everybody. And, I hope, something here to help reopen the great conversation.

Orthodoxy is an exhilarating truth that makes us happy!
"To speak of orthodoxy as a truth that makes us happy is not
always the first phrase that might come to mind because we have,
sadly, come to think of orthodox belief as a set of obligations to sign
up to, rather than a landscape to inhabit with constant amazement
and delight of the discovery opened up."
—Rowan Williams, "To What End Are We Made,"
an unpublished address, April 7, 2005

Nine Marks of Anglican Orthodoxy

Here are nine marks of "orthodoxy" as I find it in the Anglican tradition.
They will help point the way as we move through some very difficult ter-
rain—the bumpy ground of present dissension in the church and the hostil-
ity and sterility of contemporary culture.

1. Orthodoxy invites reverence before mystery and the ability to hold the
   paradox of knowing and not-knowing at the same time in silence and
   in adoration. Orthodoxy opens horizons. It invites us to a banquet. It
   does not imprison us in a fortress.

2. Orthodoxy sets limits by making a commitment to an ongoing conversation with Scripture, tradition, and one another so that we may continually be converted, following the traditional Benedictine greeting,
   "Please pray for my conversion as I pray for yours."

3. Orthodoxy makes a distinction in Scripture and tradition between
   something that actually happened and something that is given us for
   instruction—like the Genesis account of Paradise or the opening of
   the Fourth Gospel. The point of reading the Bible is for communal and
   personal transformation.

4. Orthodoxy understands, because of God's infinity and essential unknowability, that revelation in the Bible and in creation must contain an infinite multiplicity of meanings.[13]

5. Orthodoxy, therefore, requires an openness to learn something new in a spirit of generosity and to be unafraid of new knowledge.

6. Orthodoxy is convinced that doctrine is the beginning, not the end, of a conversation; knowledge of God and knowledge of self go hand in hand.

7. Orthodoxy lives within the great stories of *the revelation of God as mystery*: in the incarnation, the redemption, and the communion of the Holy and undivided Trinity, which tell us that God is with us, God loves us, God calls us—without exception—into communion.

8. Orthodoxy is committed to prayer and worship, which is the only context that makes talk about God possible, and the belief that we are never more truly ourselves than when we are gathered around one table. Anglican orthodoxy begins and ends in prayer, in silence before the mystery. It is not anti-intellectual but insists on the joining of intellect with emotion, of praying, as the Eastern tradition has it, with the mind in the heart.

9. Orthodoxy calls us to live a life of joy in the power of the resurrection as sign of hope for the world, and to serve others in the name of the one who made us and the conviction that God can be seen in everyone.

We naturally look for exemplars of Anglican orthodoxy. Henry Chadwick, the former dean of Christ Church, Oxford, sees one in Archbishop John Bramhall (d. 1663)—an exemplar of the best of the Anglican tradition. Bramhall wrote at a time when

the Church of England was a proscribed and persecuted body, when clergy who used the Prayer Book were turned out to starve and the Archbishop and the King had been executed. Bramhall regarded the Reformation as causing both good and harm. He did not regret that the English church had been set free from centralising papal jurisdiction, insensitive to the pastoral situation in England, stuffing Italians ignorant of the language into English benefices, and charging high fees. He knew that the very Catholic medieval bishop of Lincoln, Grosseteste, had declared the Roman Curia to be Antichrist.

Bramhall did not regard the papacy as antichrist (a view he associates with "Protestants out of their wits"). He "saw the Anglican position as a lonely voice of reconciliation in a polarised world called to an ecumenical task of peculiar difficulty." Bramhall wrote: "Those who understand the fewest controversies make the most and the greatest. Many differences are founded on mistakes of each other's sense. Many are mere logomachies or contentions about words. Many are merely scholastical, above the capacity and apprehension of ordinary brains."[14]

PART I

Fundamentalism and Scientism:
A Plague on Both Their Houses

Part I

Fundamentalism and Scientism:
A Plague on Both Their Houses

There's No Getting Away from "Orthodoxy"!
We should be clear that everyone has his or her own brand of "orthodoxy."
G. K. Chesterton once said something like "There are two kinds of people.
Those who believe in dogma and know it, and those who believe in dogma
and don't know it." We all have a view of the world that we tend to believe
both correct and "real." The jaundiced British spy in John le Carré's *Absolute
Friends* sarcastically points to a new orthodoxy—a new grand design for the
world.

> There's a new Grand Design about in case you haven't noticed,
> Edward. It's called preemptive naïveté, and it rests on the assumption
> that everyone in the world would like to live in Dayton, Ohio, under
> one god, no prizes for guessing whose god that is. . . . To believe that
> *God* sends you to war, *God* bends the paths of bullets, decides which of
> his children will die, or have their legs blown off, or make a hundred
> million on Wall Street, depending on today's Grand Design.[15]

But there's enough preemptive naïveté to go round. It is found as much
on the left as on the right. This, in part, is what puzzles me today—the mixture of rationalism and credulity that characterizes our age. That's not quite
right. It's more a mixture of magical thinking combined with a trust in and
reliance on technology. Fundamentalists, technologically savvy, love cell
phones as much as anyone and use the Internet well for their purposes. And
it seems to me that modern secularists are as much fundamentalists in their
own way as any Bible thumper, with a blind faith in our rational ability to
progress. A. N. Wilson in his book *After the Victorians (1901–1953)* makes the
interesting point that it was the Victorians who were able to live with doubt
and it was the weakness of the twentieth century to crave scientific and dog-

matic certainty and to believe that "if one could worry at a problem for long enough it would have a single simple solution: Keynesian or Marxist economic theory, Roman Catholic, communist, or fascist doctrine."[16] Wilson's point is a good one. Fundamentalism comes in all sizes and the longing for certainty is as strong on the left as on the right.

You can find both kinds of fundamentalist in the church. They are often called liberals and conservatives.

Sense and Sensibility—Science and Sensibility

Ian McEwan's novels often involve interplay between scientific rationalism and its inadequacy in the face of the unruly emotional life of actual human beings. For example, there are three main characters in *Enduring Love*: Joe Rose, a science journalist; Jed Parry, an obsessively religious stalker; and the "poetical" Clarissa, Joe's wife, an academic who is researching Keats. They represent the three protagonists in today's drama: the rationalist scientist, the literalist believer, and the woman of poetic sensibility. McEwan, without embracing the irrational, shows the inadequacies of the merely rational. Joe and Jed have one thing in common: they *want* to believe that everything has a point. But not everything does—some things are simply pointless. Clarissa tells her husband: "You're such a dope. You're so rational sometimes you're like a child. . . ."[17]

For Joe, on the other hand, it's no wonder that religions are spawned as "hopeful acts of propitiation, fending off mad, wild, unpredictable forces." But he's as skeptical about science as he is about religion. He thinks the typical products of the twentieth-century scientific or pseudoscientific mind are stories we make up to comfort ourselves. "Anthropology, psychoanalysis— fabulation run riot. . . . It was as though an army of white-coated Balzacs had stormed the university departments and labs."[18] Joe raises the disturbing question: Is science a narrative or not? Is science robbing the world of wonder or is the opposite true? Is religion onto something—or is it part of the pathological quest for explanation in a universe that may well be meaningless?

Joe ruminates about recent scientific writing and his wife's reaction to it all.

A few years ago, science book editors could think of nothing but chaos. Now they were banging their desks for every possible slant on neo-Darwinism, evolutionary psychology, and genetics. I wasn't complaining—business was good—but Clarissa had generally taken against the whole project. It was rationalism gone berserk. 'It's the new fundamentalism,' she said one evening. 'Twenty years ago you and your friends were all socialists and you blamed the environment on everyone's hard luck. Now you've got us trapped in our genes, and there's a reason for everything!' . . . Everything was being stripped

down, she said, and in the process some larger meaning was lost. . . .
There was nothing wrong in analyzing the bits, but it was easy to lose
sight of the whole. I agreed. The work of synthesis was crucial. Clarissa
said I didn't understand her, she was talking about love.[19]

And Jed Parry, the religious "nut" in the novel, represents a different kind
of fundamentalism and makes some good points of his own. Jed reads all of
Joe's science articles and then writes to him about Joe's views on biblical
scholarship.

[The] piece that really shocked me, [was] when you wrote about God
Himself . . . a literary character, you say, like something out of a novel.
You say the best minds in the field are prepared to take 'an educated
guess' at who invented Yahweh, that the evidence points to a woman
who was living around 1000 B.C., Bathsheba the Hittite who slept with
David. A woman novelist dreamed up God! The best minds would
rather die than to presume to know so much. . . . You write that we
know enough about chemistry these days to speculate how life began
on earth. Little mineral pools warmed by the sun, chemical bonding,
protein chains, amino acids etc. The primal soup. We've flushed God
out of this particular story, you said, and now he's being driven to his
last redoubt, among the molecules and particles of quantum physics.
But it doesn't work, Joe. Describing how the soup is made isn't the
same as knowing why it's made, or who the chef is.[20]

There's a lot of wisdom in what Jed writes, but he turns out to be danger-
ously crazy. "His world was emotion, invention and yearning."[21] But then so
is Joe's—less obvious, hidden under the veneer of rationalism.

In the middle, there's Clarissa, the poet, standing between Joe and Jed in
the Anglican position! Joe thinks his wife is dead wrong. "Clarissa thought
her emotions were an appropriate guide," he says, "that she could feel her way
to the truth, when what was needed was information, foresight, and careful
calculation."[22] But even Joe realizes that his attempt to impose order on the
universe is ridiculous. Information shouldn't be confused with communication. Joe confesses, "This patient activity brought on in me a kind of organi-
zational trance, the administrator's illusion that all the sorrow in the world
can be brought to heel with touch typing, a decent laser printer, and a box of
paper clips."

Joe sums up the present frustration with our situation:

I felt a familiar disappointment. No one could agree on anything. We
lived in a mist of half-shared, unreliable perception, and our sense data

came warped by a prism of desire and belief, which tilted our memories too. We saw and remembered in our own favor, and we persuaded ourselves along the way. Pitiless objectivity, especially about ourselves, was always a doomed social strategy. We're descended from the indignant, passionate tellers of half-truths, who, in order to convince others, simultaneously convinced themselves. Over generations success had winnowed us out, and with success came our defect, carved deep in the genes like ruts in a cart track: when it didn't suit us, we couldn't agree on what was in front of us. Believing is seeing. That's why there are divorces, border disputes, and wars, and why this statue of the Virgin Mary weeps blood and that one of Ganesh [the elephant-headed god] drinks milk. And that's why metaphysics and science were such courageous enterprises, such startling inventions, bigger than the wheel, bigger than agriculture, human artifacts set right against the grain of human nature. Disinterested truth. But it couldn't save us from ourselves, the ruts were too deep. There could be no private redemption in objectivity.[23]

Metaphysics and science, then, are courageous but doomed attempts at grasping for pure objectivity.

Seeking Mystery

McEwan nails the point about our excessive trust in our rational powers: total objectivity, he insists, especially about ourselves, is a doomed social strategy. In the light of this, Anglican tentativeness before mystery—rooted not in muddle but in awe—is a sign of strength, not weakness. There is, perhaps, one serious flaw: such an approach will never be popular or populist. Mystery doesn't sell well. Certainty does.

It's easy to see what the two fundamentalisms of science (or better, scientism) and religion have in common. While one tries to deny narrative altogether, the other takes a narrative and renders it literal. Both are seduced by the promise of pure objectivity. Both seek strategies to avoid the flawed, hit-and-miss character of human experience and history and live in an uncomplicated world of hard facts. Both tend to believe they have an exclusive hold on moral discernment. I have found in Anglicanism, as I have received it, a sane inconsistency based on deep wisdom.

At the beginning of McEwan's recent "post-9/11" novel *Saturday*, Henry Perowne, the hero, early one cold February morning contemplates his world as it wakes up to terror. He sees a plane in flames on its destructive way to Heathrow and imagines the worst. He thinks of "a man of sound faith with a bomb in the heel of his shoe" blowing up a plane and the doomed passengers praying to their god. What do they think they're doing?

[He] regards this as a matter of wonder, a human complication beyond the reach of morals. From it [faith] there spring, alongside the unreason and the slaughter, decent people and good deeds, beautiful cathedrals, mosques, cantatas, poetry. Even the denial of God, he was once amazed and indignant to hear a priest argue, is a spiritual exercise, a form of prayer: it's not easy to escape from the clutches of the believers.[24]

For the characters in this novel—and for us—there's no getting away from the questions religion poses—the basic stuff of why we're here. But what frightens or irritates believer and unbeliever alike is the nonrational or prerational aspect of our understanding of being alive and aware. Human beings, and especially those who are people of faith, find themselves in a subtle and dangerous place between the rational and irrational. And though faith comes before reason, it is not, therefore, unreasonable. The old theological maxim is "faith seeking understanding." That means that rational discourse is important—in fact, vital—but only as a way of understanding something we have already apprehended, not comprehended, by faith. Many of us believe it's worth getting up in the morning and, while we cannot *prove* it, we can demonstrate that it's *reasonable*. Sound faith, then, presupposes rational discourse, the ability to share in debate, and to participate in a never-ending conversation about purpose and meaning. Immature faith, on the other hand, is trust in propositions—a kind of magical thinking about words as such and the conviction that we can grasp and package reality. But what everyone's looking for, after all—the natural human response—is a place of light and safety, a secure high ground.

Light and Safety

Are we in a new Dark Ages or are we awaiting the approaching dawn? As we search for that place of light and safety, many of us are looking for "right belief"—orthodoxy—in the face of the failure and bankruptcy of secularism and an increasingly trashy culture. The frustrated person of faith is likely to be someone with a bomb in the heel of his shoe—if not literally then metaphorically. It seems as if more and more people are getting to the point of nonnegotiability even to the point of being addicted to polarization.

One "solution" to bring light to the religious darkness is secular rationalism. The alarmed and often arrogant "rationalist" might be busy making bombs of his own. There are people of deep conviction who are faithful atheists. Consider, for example, Richard Dawkins, who carries his unbelief before him like a banner. A professor for the Public Understanding of Science at Oxford, Dawkins is best known for a couple of books—*The Selfish Gene* and *The Blind Watchmaker*. His objection to religious belief is of the Monty Python "What about the Spanish Inquisition?" school: Religion is a bad thing because it devalues human life and breeds violence. Setting religion loose on the world, he contends, is like littering the street with guns, and subscribing to religion is nothing but infantile regression—like believing the earth is flat or in the existence of unicorns. "Religions in general," Dawkins says, "teach people not to think for themselves, but to be satisfied with handed-down, authoritarian, traditional wisdom, never based on evidence."[25]

But believers don't have a monopoly on infantile thinking. Nor are they the only ones who resort to violence. Don't all ideologically driven people—including atheists—tend not to think for themselves? And can we lay violence only at the feet of churchgoers? It has been reckoned that between 85 and 100 million were slaughtered in the last century by "atheists."[26]

Other atheists are less testy and more affable than Dawkins, like Daniel Dennett, who likens religious believers to Dumbo, the little elephant of Disney's 1941 cartoon, who was taunted because of his enormous ears and believed he could fly because of a "magic" feather. He is too young to understand what the laughter is about, but old enough to know that it's aimed at him. Cruelly separated from his mother by the circus, misunderstood and mistreated by the other animals, he's all alone in the world with "no warm trunk to cuddle up to, no one to dry his tears." Fortunately, he's got someone in his corner—Timothy Mouse. With his new friend's help and guidance, Dumbo has the courage to take a leap of faith that turns the taunting into cheers and makes all his dreams soar.

At the heart of the story, though, there's a deception—a useful one, but a deception all the same. Dumbo is being encouraged by his friends the crows to leap off a cliff into the air, proving to himself that he can fly. Dumbo is understandably reluctant. One crow has a bright idea. When Dumbo isn't looking, he plucks a tail feather and hands it to Dumbo, telling him it's magic. Dumbo clutches it in his trunk—believes in the magic, and flies.

For many people, religion functions a bit like that magic feather. It comforts but it doesn't really signify anything. But Dennett himself also believes in a kind of magic. He believes that four and a half billion years ago the planet was lifeless, "and *then life emerged*" (emphasis mine). Just like that. Perhaps that's materialism's magic feather—the prerational leap of faith that life just happens? Here's the nub of the argument. Is it more reasonable to suppose that life "just happened" or to believe that life has direction and purpose that we can only partially fathom? Neither position can be proved. Each side thinks, however, that its position is more reasonable than the other's.

Professor Dennett urges us to grow up and grow out of religion by trading in mysteries for mechanisms. It's true that we all need to grow up, but I think growing up involves making more and more room for mystery and giving up the magical thinking that somehow mechanisms will save us.

There's a distinguished tradition of "learned ignorance" (an intelligent and informed not-knowing) that needs to be revived by the partisans on all sides. We cannot live without stories and myths. Science alone isn't enough. Since the testing and dropping of the atom bomb in 1945, science lost its claim to innocence. There is no such thing as "just research." No one is outside the drama of human striving and suffering.

Telling Our Stories
Our stories are essential to us. Even the assertion that there is no story is a story. As William of Baskerville, Umberto Eco's detective in *The Name of the Rose*, states, "There was no plot and I discovered it by mistake." C. G. Jung wrote: Anyone "who thinks he can live without myth, or outside it, like one uprooted, has no true link either with the past, or with the ancestral life which continues within him, or yet of contemporary human society. This plaything of his reason never grips his vitals."[27]

We all like secure answers to our deepest questions. We all look for assurance with regard to our fears and obsessions. And the answers and assurances, more often than not, come to us in the form of a story or a myth. Even science needs a story. The heart of the narrative takes on many forms and is expressed in such things as homeschooling for some Evangelicals to the revival of the Latin Mass for some Roman Catholics. Behind the homeschooling movement there is a story about a world that has lost its way. For some Roman Catholics, the Latin Mass represents the ordered transcendence of a former age. There is nothing wrong with either. Each story tells us about a place of safety and depth.

Desperately Seeking Orthodoxy
Whenever we come to a place of safety and settling, we call it "orthodoxy"— right belief. "Orthodoxy" of whatever stripe becomes an anchor for the tempest-tossed. No matter where you land on the political and religious continuum, you have the satisfaction of knowing you are right. You are orthodox.

"Orthodoxy" or right belief is one of those subjects that need careful handling because it is often a place where bomb makers hide. Christian orthodoxy is claimed by two kinds of believers: the noisiest are those who see it as the acceptance and affirmation of *propositions* in creeds, texts, and doctrines. In effect, they are rationalists. For them, orthodoxy requires verbal assent to certain statements. At the extreme it is thought that, should Osama bin Laden on his deathbed accept Jesus Christ as his personal Lord and Savior, he will go straight to heaven, while faithful and compassionate non-Christians will go to the other place no matter what. There is no doubt in my mind that a repentant terrorist can go to heaven, but the kind of orthodoxy that takes no account of the moral life but only of verbal assent is obscene.

Judgment is a mystery and we leave it to God to judge between a hateful Christian and a Christlike atheist.

We cannot avoid the dark truth that Christianity, with Judaism and Islam, is marred and marked by violence. The chief rabbi of England, Jonathan Sacks, reminds us, "the first recorded act of religious worship leads directly to the first murder."[28] Cain kills Abel. And Father Timothy Radcliffe comments, "The Exodus of Israel leaves the firstborn of Egypt dead in their beds and their warriors drowned on the seashore. The Christian story climaxes in a brutal execution. Our faiths cannot be sanitized."[29] The question is: How can we tell these stories in a way that does no violence to others? We tend to take refuge in the superiority of our narrative and think of others as merely characters in *our* story. Father Radcliffe disturbingly suggests that "it belongs to the proper telling of our Christian story that it is not the only story to tell."[30]

Devotion to verbal formulas, absolute certainty, and narrative superiority infects both conservatives and liberals. Both sides are obsessed with being correct. Others, both conservatives and liberals (and I am among them)— seeing the limits of the rationalist approach—follow a second way of understanding orthodoxy that begins with the awesome mystery of God, which cannot be put into words. For us—since we cannot do without them—the great doctrines enshrined in the ancient creeds initiate a never-ending conversation, a journey into mystery. These established creeds lead us to contemplate the birth of Jesus from Mary his mother (the incarnation), the broken and ruined man on the cross whose self-giving love shows us the heart of God and brings us home to God and to each other (the redemption), and the communion of persons as the revelation of complete unity in amazing diversity (the Trinity). All these great doctrines are immensely *practical*. They have implications with regard to character and behavior. They impinge on our political affiliations and social arrangements.

Christian orthodoxy, therefore, looks at the world through the prism of the three basic doctrines of incarnation, redemption, and communion. And Christian orthodoxy demands a moral response. Since we can say true things falsely, the test of anyone's orthodoxy lies in orthopraxis (right behavior) in the moral life. Right believing results in the development of a certain kind of character. You cannot love God and hate your brother or sister. Worship (especially the Eucharist) and prayer are central in this understanding of orthodoxy. Faith, in the end, isn't *argument*; it's adoration.

The Anglican Tradition of Orthodoxy

The Anglican tradition, at its best, has tended to embrace this second way of understanding orthodoxy as affirming a mystery that elicits worship and eludes our attempts to pin it down in mere words. This approach is not the property of any party or tribe. Rather, it's a mind-set found among conservatives and liberals, Catholics and Protestants—just as the rationalist propositional mind-set is found in all factions and parties.

We used to be able to talk to each other but now the conversation is falling apart. For Anglicans, this is more serious than for those who belong to more dogmatic or "confessional" churches. Roman Catholics appeal to the *magisterium*, and many Protestants appeal to "the inerrancy of Scripture"— two problematic forms of infallibility, neither of which sets a high value on conversation.

Some years ago, after my preaching in a suburban church just outside San Francisco, a woman—who hated the new Prayer Book, couldn't take women priests, and found homosexuals beyond the pale—cornered me during coffee hour. "Before you people came along with this Prayer Book, these women, and these homosexuals," she lamented, "we had this darling little church." She clung to the vision of the unchanging "orthodoxy" of her childhood. But that darling little church has disappeared forever (if it ever really existed in the first place) and we are in the whirlwind of hurt, controversy, and change. And it's no wonder. The brave new world of modernity didn't materialize. Because the secular project has failed, many live in a howling spiritual vacuum, which advocates of new and old orthodoxies are eager to fill. Some of us (I pray for a critical mass) seek to be obedient to an *open* tradition; that is, a tradition which passes on life and is not mere repetition of what has gone before.

We should be encouraged by the fact that the church, after all, has never been the gathering together of the like-minded. As Peter Carnley, the retired primate of Australia, puts it:

> Christianity does not involve the gathering of people around some kind of beautiful idea that is uniformly shared. We come together as Christians not because we recognize one another as entertaining the same mind-set . . . Rather, Christians are drawn together for no reason other than they are called together by the Word of God . . . the person of Jesus Christ.[31]

The trouble is that we—conservatives and liberals and all of us in between—have become idiots (in the technical sense of that word). We have lost any sense of that *shared* call. Let me explain. Here's an example from the ancient Romans:

> If one word sums up the general difference between us and the Romans—it is *public*. . . . The very term *republic* (the "public thing") incorporates the word. The horrors of 20th-century collectivism have left us with a reasonable suspicion of coerced community. Even so, the

contemporary eclipse of the public and accessible in literature, art, and philosophy by the private and idiosyncratic would have been considered a disaster by the Romans as well as the Greeks. Our term *idiot* comes from the Latin *idiota*, an adaptation of the Greek *idiotes*, which means "private person."[32]

Behind all the disputes and divisions lies this kind of idiocy. We are unable to listen and pay attention to one another. We tend to talk only to the like-minded and shout at or demonize those who differ from us. Hence our often inept, facile, arrogant, and thin talk about God. There is no group—right, left, or middle—that isn't subject to this idiocy. So before we get to all those things that have undermined our darling little church, we need to recover some sense of revelation and authority, continuity and innovation in the light of God's ineffable mystery.

The Mystery of God at the Heart of Orthodoxy

All this has led me to attempt a definition of Anglican orthodoxy based on the tradition as I have received it. It's no accident that the mystics called the Christian life the school of love, and Archbishop Rowan Williams has described the church as providing *schooling* in conversation.

Where else to begin a discussion of Christian orthodoxy but with the doctrine of God? Let's take a brief look at Rowan Williams's theology—and his critics—to recover this doctrine. Williams has been accused, by the group I call the propositionally orthodox, of having no theology of revelation at all. The reason for this assessment is that the archbishop places himself firmly in the Eastern Orthodox apophatic tradition, which insists on the centrality of the mystery of God. Take, for example, the archbishop's use of the Christ child as a revelation of God's character. Mary gives birth to the Word who cannot speak! "Ask a baby about the ordination of women," Williams writes, "about divorce. . . , violence on television, who will win the election: it is not a fruitful experience."[33] We are met with silence. The Word does not speak. Imagine holding a baby in your arms and asking it, "What do you think about stem cell research? What's your take on gay marriage? What would you have done in the Terry Schiavo case?" As we're compelled to do when we gaze at the image of Mary holding the silent infant Word, in all our conversations—no matter what side we're on—we must begin with silence and a commitment to listen to one another.

But often we speak too quickly. Many of us are pushed into declaring a position when, in fact, our thoughts are unformed. We are called upon to take sides prematurely. I can sympathize with the frustration on both sides—the slow thinkers who need time as well as those impatient with the fence-sitters, who think that time is running out.

With the Gene Robinson case—the ordination of a gay bishop in New Hampshire—this silence before the mystery of God would have stood all of us in good stead. Should Bishop Gene Robinson and his supporters have exercised patience and restraint in the face of African sensibility and consciousness? Is schism too high a price to pay for having an openly gay bishop in the Episcopal Church? This kind of argument can drive liberals mad. "Justice cannot be delayed!" they insist. "The time is now." Well, some of us are a bit slow. We ask awkward questions. We counsel the virtues of forbearance and patience and understand that if everyone pushed his claims to the limit we'd all be against the wall and life would be unbearable. Why do we—liberals and conservatives—insist that everyone march to the beat of our particular drum? New Hampshire is a long way from Lagos. Africa, after all, has its own challenges to and deviations from the tradition. The cultural norms are different, and so is the approach to tradition and Scripture. Why can't both sides talk and listen to each other?

There are other contentious issues, too, and we don't have to look too far back to find them. Why, for example, couldn't the old Book of Common Prayer be authorized alongside the new? After all, the individual churches in the Anglican communion use more than one Prayer Book (and some, to my distress, don't appear to use one at all). Why do we need ecclesiastical legislation to make people comply when practice, custom, and use are better methods? If you're going to be part of something really big, you're going to have to put up with it moving slowly and be prepared for things you don't like. You're going to have to be open to both those who seem painfully slow and those who rush ahead.

Here's another example: At Grace Cathedral, San Francisco, we use a fraction anthem adapted from the one used at St. James's, Piccadilly, in London. It mentions Jews, Muslims, Buddhists, Hindus, and all "those who walk the way of faith." We break the bread for the whole world. We also invite "all who seek God and are drawn to Christ" to the table. The vast majority of people who experience our rather traditional liturgy are deeply moved by its generous inclusiveness. A few are shocked and offended by it and for two reasons: One, it seems mindlessly indiscriminate, and two, it is in violation of the rubrics of the Book of Common Prayer. I take these two criticisms very seriously. With regard to the first objection, we point to the ongoing conversation in the church about who is included and who isn't. We only offer this as an experiment worthy of dialogue and discussion. We also point out that it isn't advocating a total openness. Those invited have to be seeking God and drawn to Christ. Our experience has been that our Christian formation programs are oversubscribed and we have more and more adult baptisms. With regard to the second objection, we may be wrong. We are open to correction. We long for civil and, if need be, contentious conversation. Good theology is

dialectical. No one has the last word. For some people, we are too traditional, for others, too "far out." We seek, especially in these times, the not-to-be-
despised middle ground. We seek always to listen to one another in silence
before the mystery of God. I confess that I'm not always good about listening in patience and silence. I am driven to distraction by the Eastern
Orthodox mentality that promises we might be able to share communion
but it might take a thousand years. And questions of justice, of course, cannot be ignored. It's deeply immoral and offensive to ask African Americans
to keep on riding at the back of the bus for a few more years, to ask women
to "know their place" just a little longer, to ask gay people to stay in the closet and keep quiet for another decade. Such requests are unacceptable, but if
each of us were to push our claims to the limit, life would be impossible.

It may be that we overstate the challenge of the gay bishop of New
Hampshire. There are, to my mind, deeper things for concern. There is a
spirit alive and well in the Anglican Communion as seen in the Australian
Diocese of Sydney where "theological hatred" (*Odium theologicum*) "is part
of the culture—exemplified by Dean Phillip Jensen [of Sydney Cathedral]
calling non-Christian religions 'monstrous lies and deceits of Satan' and
writing of Roman Catholicism, despite Vatican II, as an organization that continues to be "sub-Christian in its doctrine and practice." So interfaith dialogue
and ecumenism are a waste of time—they distract from the more urgent task
of evangelism and indeed may soften one up for doctrinal corruption.[34] One
wonders if Sydney Anglicans care about the Communion at all?

A community—a communion—requires some measure of personal vol-
untary restraint. It's not surprising that we may well find ourselves on different sides of a great divide on a particular issue. This is no excuse to break
communion or demonize the other. Sometimes the only places we can meet
are in the silence and at the table (and, alas, for some, not even there).

I come back again and again to the image of Mary and her baby Son—
the image of the Word who cannot speak as an icon for our time. A picture,
as they say, is worth a thousand words. The painting *La Madonna del Parto*
(c. 1460) by Piero della Francesca is on the wall of the church of Santa Maria
a Nomentana at Monterchi, near Arezzo in Italy. Mary is standing, wearing a
blue dress, with her right hand pointing downward at a long split in the
dress, indicating her pregnancy. Her left hand is on her hip and her facial
expression is ambiguous—boredom, serenity, indifference, resignation,
acceptance? Above her is a canopy held open by two angels. The canopy is a
reminder of the ark of the Old Covenant (Exodus 26:7), the sign of God's
dwelling among us. Mary is the Ark of the New Covenant protecting in her
womb the Son of God. In this way Mary is a sign of the church—the body of
Christ—the place where God dwells. It is said that the artist meditated on the
sacred silence of Mary when he painted this picture.

Silence is a vital concept in the Christian tradition. Our tradition speaks of the contemplation of the silence of the Virgin concerning the secret of God. It also speaks of the mute Mother of the silent Word, which is echoed in the words of St. John of the Cross: "The Father utters one Word and that Word is his Son and he utters him forever in everlasting silence, and in silence the soul has to hear him." This reverence for mystery is at the heart of Anglican orthodoxy. The Word that erupts out of silence and returns to silence is a key to the true understanding of theology and, by extension, to our self-understanding. We need words and words fail us. "The heart has reasons of which reason knows nothing" (Blaise Pascal). Theology is best done—indeed can only be done—on our knees.

A Theology of Transcendent Mystery

This way of talking about God is difficult or even unacceptable to some Anglicans, especially to certain Evangelicals, because it appears to be a theology that negates all theologies. It seems to be a retreat from speech into darkness. But for those of us (like the archbishops Rowan Williams, Peter Carnley, Michael Ramsey, and Robert Runcie) who find encouragement in the tradition of the Eastern Church, God is *revealed* as transcendent mystery—a God who will not be contained in human concepts. Peter Carnley rightly suggests that this points "to one of the most profound differences of opinion within contemporary Anglicanism."[35] It isn't a matter of left or right, or conservative or liberal. The split is right down the middle of each party. Liberals find it just as hard to endure the silence and mystery of God as conservatives do. On the other hand, there are those on both sides who struggle to wait together in that silence. Those of a conservative mind who think of revelation in terms of a body of information of a propositional kind find it in the pages of Scripture. The liberals find revelation in a kind of consensus of modern consciousness. God's will is all perfectly clear—and profoundly different—to both sides.

Peter Carnley writes,

> Others of us, in contrast, appreciate the Word of God not so much as a body of information, but as a form of questioning of the inner motives of our hearts, or as an invitation to relate with God, who ultimately remains essentially an unfathomable mystery to us, and as a Word of promise to be with us always as we wrestle to discern his truth for the living of our lives.[36]

What is both serious and sad is that so many of us—at odds about our theologies—have ceased to try to talk to one another. Instead, we do a lot of name-calling. People on both sides are like the Donatists, those superior, self-confident Christians so roundly condemned by St. Augustine. The Donatists, he declared, were like frogs "who grunt from their little pond: 'Christians? None but us.'"[37] The question posed in Augustine's time is as relevant now as it was in the fourth or fifth century: Is the church a school of perfection or a hospital for sinners? Of course it is both. But the modern church, both liberal and conservative, is more Donatist—more either-or—than Augustinian.

So in the face of all this contentious and self-righteous squabbling, the recovery of "orthodoxy" requires us to sit before the mystery of God in silence and only then to speak. We are called to recover the art of godly conversation. But many of us have forgotten the "rules" for talking to one another about the life of faith. Some of us have given up and have taken refuge in an "idiotic" tribalism, adopting a strident rhetoric as a substitute for civil discourse. And in my pessimistic mood I tend to agree with the prophetic imagination of Dostoyevsky, who saw the emergence of a society of men and women without any sense of good and evil, without manners, without any elementary piety or prejudices—"groups of venomous, self-assertive individuals, shameless in their rudeness, unembarrassed in their contradictory but despotic denunciations."[38]

The Anglican Conversation Today

Into this fray steps Rowan Williams, to my mind a great archbishop whose job must be hell. He is a contemplative, an independent, and a traditionalist who knows that in a higher world it is otherwise, but here below "to live is to change and to be perfect is to have changed often."[39] We have a liberal archbishop who is committed to the tradition. Think about that: He will never be pleasing to the extremes but will bring many of us together. What a job! I am much encouraged by his ministry. As an English bishop said to me: "With the appointment of Rowan Williams we can at last *think* again!"

When the Anglican Consultative Council met in Nottingham, England, in June 2005, the mood wasn't exactly conciliatory. "The Episcopal Church was said to have almost groveled before the delegates. There's a sense that this moment is payback time after years of being patronized."[40] But there are 77 million Anglicans, the majority of whom simply try to live the Christian life. Meanwhile, though, conservative leaders are on the march. The archbishop of Canterbury, "acutely aware of the spectacle the Church is making of itself over its obsession with an issue which at best affects only a small minority," told the delegates, "Here is a group of Christians talking to each other, they will think, arguing over matters that seem quite a long way from the plight of a child soldier in northern Uganda or a mother with HIV/AIDS in Lesotho, or a sweatshop worker or fisherman in south Asia. Some will react with contempt—what a parade of foolish anger, bigotry and self-importance, what a fuss over the 'rights' of the prosperous. . . ." And then comments one reporter, "within hours on an American website, a US conservative was denouncing Dr. Williams as no better than a left-wing agnostic." What's happening? That particular conservative must know such an assertion is a lie. So we wait now for the emergence of the Anglican Global Initiative as it sets up a church within a church. We seem determined to think the worst of each other.

Fundamental but Not Fundamentalist

Yet I am also encouraged because we may be able to affirm some basic Christian fundamentals without being fundamentalist. We have to give up the claustrophobic comforts of sectarian religion—where there is no questioning and no doubts and everyone marches along in a lockstep. This is called theocracy—the rule of God—and it assumes that there can be an end to dialogue and discovery. That's why it's so attractive. Some believers, if they had their way, would outlaw unbelief. They assume, says the archbishop, "that there could be a situation in which believers in effect had nothing to learn . . . the gift of a time of repentance and growth are set aside."[41] But it is this need for change, growth, and repentance that saves the person of faith from being a tyrant. This is the gracious work of the Holy Spirit. That's a fundamental and it is one that I heartily endorse.

We Anglicans have other fundamentals. They have to do as much with the *way* we believe as with *what* we believe. Not long after the announcement of Williams's appointment as the new archbishop of Canterbury, there was a flurry of news flashes about lots of clergy in England not believing in the Bible or the creeds in a literal way. A report from a conservative group funded from a U.S. legacy found that a large number of clergy (and more women than men) didn't believe the doctrines of the church *literally*. The implication was that you either believe these literally or not at all—there's no fudging, as if the past two hundred years or so of intellectual life in the church hadn't happened. Clergy who didn't believe literally were accused of hypocrisy. The *London Times* for August 1, 2002, ran a section on believing literally in the virgin birth and in the resurrection. It included two articles by two Church of England clergymen, writing at cross-purposes. Newspaper editors love this. "Are the pulpits of Anglican Churches occupied by closet atheists?" they inquired. Wow! I believe the Bible and the creed, but not literally—and I am no atheist. I have a great devotion to Mary the Mother of God but am agnostic about her literal virginity. The point of the doctrine is not to teach us about Mary's sexual status but to show us the awesome humility and availability of God. That's what the doctrine is for. That's what it's about. As I have already confessed, every day I invoke the protection of the holy angels, but I hear no flapping of wings. Belief in angels is a way for me to affirm the presence of God in a personal way permeating the whole of life. We need poetry and metaphor to express these great mysteries. Christian Wiman, editor of *Poetry Magazine*, puts it well: "Let us remember . . . that in the end we go to poetry for one reason, so that we might more fully inhabit our lives and the world in which we live them, and that if we more fully inhabit these things, we might be less apt to destroy both."[42]

Nigel Williams's hero in his novel *Witchcraft* complains, "My father was a vicar . . . One of those new vicars, who don't believe in God or evil or any of that rubbish. Who thinks RESURRECTION is a novel by Tolstoy."[43] It's as if we are presented with only two options: the evangelical one and the progressive one. Some of us don't think it's a good idea to make it up as you go along. I'm not drawn to a form of Christianity in which

> Jesus Christ is no longer the Son of God, the second Person of the Trinity, the redeemer, but one of the many gateways into the realm of God. The Lord's Supper is not a sharing in the body and blood of Christ, but a ritual meal that projects the vision of world peace. The Church is not to be defined by standards of belief, but should equally embrace believers and agnostics. It is a community in which doctrines and beliefs are simply not very important and where questions are more important than answers. This may appeal to those with answers they found uncongenial.[44]

But neither can I take these polarities seriously. An Anglican question, so puzzling to the polarized, is this: Why can't both be true? Why can't the Eucharist be both a sharing in the body and blood of Christ *and* a ritual meal that projects the vision of world peace?

The "radical orthodox" theologian John Millbank tells us,

> I'm used to people saying, "Do you really believe in the virgin birth?"or the Resurrection, the miracles, these things that modernity rejected. I would say, "Yes, of course, we believe." But what we're saying is that this story is a complex theological statement that none of us fully understands. The idea that it's nonsense, that it doesn't fit secular principles, is in itself a secular form of knowledge. The virgin birth is not just a metaphor. Calling it a myth, or a metaphor, assumes objective knowledge which we don't have.[45]

But you have to call it something. Huston Smith suggests that the metaphor of "modernity"—the idea of endless progress through science-powered technology—is dead. "It is only cultural lag—the backward pull of the outgrown good—that keeps us running on it."[46] And if modernism is dead, so is the kind of postmodernism that derides and denies any meta- or grand narrative. It cannot imagine a metanarrative that wouldn't be totalitarian. So it rejects "story" altogether. Minimalism leads to nihilism. There is no consensual worldview holding us all together—which has its good side, because it mitigates marginalizing people. The postmodernist insists that we have no reliable maps and we don't know how to make them. Philosopher Richard Rorty tells us, "There is no big picture." But this itself becomes the story. The story is that there is no big-picture story. We might ask, "Is this reductionism?" Does this reduce all our attempts to tell a meaningful story to nothing? No, says Rorty, because there's nothing to reduce.

The wonder of Christianity, albeit often betrayed by Christians, is the non-oppressive principle of the cross. The cross coerces and oppresses no one. It turns our idea of power upside down. Ours is a narrative that is capable of constant revision. Postmodernists often overlook that their story—there is no story—can be oppressive and even totalitarian.

That's why I think of myself as a conservative, because I refuse to give up what some others deride as "primitive." I know that I cannot live without or outside a story. We seem wired to need some kind of big picture. Claude Levi-Strauss tells us that the deepest difference between the epistemology of traditional peoples and ours is that "primitives" believe that you cannot understand anything unless you understand *everything*. Levi-Strauss thought traditional peoples were wrong but Huston Smith thinks they were exactly right and I agree with him. A vision of the whole and communion within it is built into the fabric of things. As Smith observes, we don't have or take time for the larger view. "With us, life's problems press so heavily on us that we seldom take time to reflect on the way our unconscious attitudes and assumptions about the nature of things affect the way we perceive what is directly before us."[47] The big-picture view requires us to take note of the background of our lives—the backdrop. Is it the sacred canopy or the market? Smith's view is that the traditional worldview is preferable because it allows for the fulfillment of the basic longing that lies in the depths of the human heart. The notion that people before us were children in comparison with us has been shown to be absurd.

To make his point, Huston Smith quotes a poem by Stephen Dunn, "At the Smithville Methodist Church," about a child who comes home wearing a "Jesus Saves" button after an arts-and-crafts week. The parents want to be honest with their daughter but they can't bring themselves to tell her that Jesus doesn't love her. So they keep quiet.

> It had been so long since we believed, so long
> since we needed Jesus
> as our nemesis and friend, that we thought he was
> sufficiently dead,

that our children would think of him like Lincoln
or Thomas Jefferson.
Soon it became clear to us: you cannot teach disbelief
to a child,

only wonderful stories, and we hadn't a story
        nearly as good.

. . . .

You can't say to your child
"Evolution loves you." The story stinks
of extinction and nothing

exciting happens for centuries. I didn't have
a wonderful story for my child
and she was beaming. All the way home in the car
she sang the songs,

occasionally standing up for Jesus.
There was nothing to do
but drive, ride it out, sing along
in silence.[48]

Religion simply won't go away. It's not about to disappear. Children need
stories that don't stink of extinction—not for sentimental reasons, but
because nihilism is unreasonable. When Huston Smith returned to his childhood haunts in China, he arrived at church forty minutes early to standing
room only. The pastor pleaded with the congregation not to attend church
more than once each Sunday to give others a chance. He heard stories of the
Cultural Revolution—of Christians being forced to wear dunce caps and
kneel for two hours on broken glass in front of jeering mobs. He realized that
no amount of repression can destroy our wiring for God. We may be silent,
but we sing along all the same.

Conservative and Liberal Perspectives

This highlights the weakness of liberalism. It is an effort—sometimes noble and
heroic—to dispense with tradition and ancient ways of believing. Smith writes,

Liberals are at their worst in not recognizing how much an absolute
can contribute to life, and in assuming that absolutes can be held only
dogmatically, which is not the case. Absolutism and dogmatism lie on
different axes. The first relates to belief, whereas the second is a char-

acter disorder. The opposite of absolutism is not open-mindedness but relativism, and the opposite of dogmatism is not relativism but open-mindedness. There can be, and are dogmatic relativists and open-minded absolutists.[49]

But, he goes on,

liberals [are] better than conservatives at recognizing the dangers of fanaticism and the virtues of tolerance, and conservatives [are] better at perceiving the dangers of nihilism and the virtues of a sense of certainty. . . . Both the strengths and dangers of liberalism pertain to life's horizontal dimension, which encompass[es] human relationships—whereas those of conservatives pertain to the vertical, asymmetrical God-person relationship.[50]

Liberals need to learn that the vertical relation is more important. It seems to me that the conservative diagnosis is often right but its remedy (charging back into an idealized and imagined past) is both unworkable and disastrous. The liberal is often a poor diagnostician but, at least, has an inkling of freedom in God.

The liberal and conservative battle is parodied in Michael Arditti's novel, *Easter*. The bishop is a hearty Evangelical; the archdeacon a bigoted Anglo-Catholic: "The Bishop finds God in the pages of the Bible like a lazy schoolboy cribbing for an exam; the Archdeacon finds God in a ritual meal the way the primitive warriors ate their dead chiefs." Arditti launched a stout defense of Anglican liberalism. The creed of the protagonist, he insists,

has become a paradox: "I doubt therefore I believe", the cri de coeur of twentieth-century liberalism. No wonder the evangelicals find it easy to pour scorn. How much simpler it must be to locate salvation in the utilitarian prose of their New International Bibles, to read myths as though they were history and history as though they heard it on the news. Meanwhile, liberalism limps on, as decimated in the Church as in politics: a weak third force trying to hold its own between the two rival wings of doctrinaire Catholicism and fundamentalism. And yet it is far more than his personal belief that is at stake, for liberalism has always been the quintessential English virtue—the philosophical equivalent of decency and fair play.[51]

The bishop thinks that "a liberal Christian is a contradiction in terms, because liberals believe in asking questions, to which Christians already have the answers. If you don't believe me, you haven't read your Bible."[52]

The difference between the two is summed up near the end of the novel. "The truth is that Christ became incarnate not to redeem a sinful people who had cut themselves off from salvation, but to reassure a suffering people of their unity with God. Or, to put it another way, the world was not in a state of sin waiting for Christ to rescue it; the world is in a state of grace, waiting for us to recognize it."[53] Of course, as an Anglican, I'd say that both statements are true! It's a matter of emphasis. Polarization is a form of indulgence and is both unnecessary and harmful. The world is in both a state of sin and a state of grace. Human beings are both fallen and free.

Celebrating Communion

Friendship can go a long way toward healing differences. Friendship, too, is a way of doing theology. Here's a story about the friendship between an Anglican and a Roman Catholic priest. On June 17, 1999, Father François Legaux, the rector of the Cathedral of Our Lady of Chartres, was installed as an honorary canon of Grace Cathedral in San Francisco. It was not only a significant ecumenical event but also an affirmation that what we have in common far outweighs our differences. This celebration of the relationship between two pilgrimage cathedrals was also a sign of mutual respect and affection between our two communions. It was a matter of falling in love. A year later, I was installed as honorary canon of Chartres cathedral.

Meanwhile, another significant event took place at around the same time. It was the publication of *The Gift of Authority* by the Anglican–Roman Catholic International Commission (ARCIC)—a bit of a bombshell (a much-needed one, to my mind) affirming that our two communions could come closer together under the primacy of Peter, radically reinterpreted. Some evangelical Anglicans see this report as a betrayal of the Reformation. Some Roman Catholics see it as a betrayal of the principle of unequivocal submission to the see of Rome. But the document raises the question of the mess of history and how we live in and through it. The subtext of the document—totally unacknowledged as far I can tell—is that authority as currently practiced in our two traditions simply isn't working. Father Legaux said, in his address at his installation, that to advance toward unity requires deep prayer and is tested by

> the quality of our love for one another. The ruptures in the Church, over the course of its history, have been a great evil. No one can deny this. Because God alone is capable of drawing good from evil, our separations have, over the course of the centuries, permitted the enrichment of each confession by its own history and its own culture. But above all, the Holy Spirit has been given to each of our communions as a witness to the diversity of the riches we share in God. This is why the future of our unity cannot be a simple return to what was com-

mon before. We cannot reunite ourselves, in truth, unless we accept the differences of each other as an enrichment of ourselves. Unity is the fruit of prayer and must be lived out in love.

Father Legaux concluded his short address with these words: "History made us who we are. Now it is up to us to make history as we hope it will be." This expresses the tension of living in time and space and affirms the work of the Spirit in and through our differences for our mutual enrichment. History, not eternity, is the theater of the Spirit and, for the most part, we don't like it. The Reformation happened, and so did the Counter-Reformation. The question now is, "So what?"

So the more important question is, "What do we do now? How do we respond to the Spirit now?" This, of course, drives us beyond issues of the differences between Rome and Canterbury, beyond the differences between the various denominations, even beyond issues of relations between the great religious traditions. This question drives us, once again, to reflect on the very nature of God and of humanity. It compels us to think long and hard, and to ask ourselves: "What is Christianity really about?" The Spirit is calling us out of our tribal and national manifestations into a way of being in the world that truly expresses the universal good news of love and reconciliation.

Living in the Mess of History

The Spirit is teaching us that we live in the mess of history. There is no unchanging human nature. We are called into a pilgrim community, through the saving images of Scripture, to joyfully celebrate God's hospitality in a community where the unqualified and the rejected are the most welcome. We are invited to fall in love. To put it another way: The theater of the Spirit is history, which means that we are in an endless conversation with mystery of what it is to be human in the context of thrilling images of love and mercy in a community centered around a table from which no one is excluded. These images and the eucharistic table set the political and social agenda for our being in the world.

The church then might be a place for adventurers of the Spirit rather than the refuge of the frightened in a kind of boutique Anglicanism or a rigidly certain and dying Roman Catholicism. History tells us again and again that the world has suffered greatly from immature, violent, vindictive, fearful, tribal religion. But the Holy Spirit invites us to choose gratitude over resentment, to embrace a banquet rather than a fortress. This means giving up our judgmentalism and joining in God's indiscriminate taste in loving everyone, even the desperately wicked.

The relationship Grace Cathedral has with Chartres is a sign of many things: the friendship between two priests of different communions; the fact that Roman Catholicism isn't as coherent a system as some people think; the way personal contacts can leapfrog over differences so that a liberal Catholic cathedral in the Anglican tradition can celebrate its relationship with one of the most distinguished cathedrals in the West and bypass the infighting within Anglicanism.

The Spirit is always at work. History has brought us now to a situation where the divisions are not so much between the traditions as within them. I have more in common with a French Roman Catholic than with many Anglican liberals, on the one hand, and the ultraconservative group of Anglicans on the other. I find I live more in the world of the Roman Catholic weekly *The Tablet* than in any Anglican journal. The issue has to do with the world we actually live in, not the world as we would like it to be. The issue is about history and the faithless attempt to invoke an orthodoxy that never really existed in history. The Spirit's theater is history—messy, inconclusive, provisional. The Spirit calls us to faith and trust, not to rigid tribal certainties. Does the Spirit call us to a God who is inviting, calling, attracting, or to one who is controlling, directing, regulating? Again, the polarization is as untruthful as it is unnecessary. The Spirit directs and regulates by calling and attracting. It is not a matter of either-or. The Spirit calls us to a God who Father Andrew Greeley insists charms us. What a thought! A God who charms, who longs for us. We need to do for dogma what we have struggled to do with Scripture—to repudiate literalism and recover the poetic, mythic, metaphorical, and playful use of the imagination so that the beauty of holiness may reappear.

The Spirit, Alive and Loose

I am struck over and over again by how the churches protect the tradition instead of letting it loose. I make no claims for Grace Cathedral in San Francisco. Just like everyone else, we are sinners. We resist the Spirit and avoid risk as much as possible. But we are, whether we like it or not, at one of the great crossroads of the world. I have the privilege of being part of a community dedicated to daily prayer. This ground base of prayer, coupled with the lively glory and tragedy of living in a modern city, bring together the two aspects of the work of the Spirit—the still small voice and its wind and fire. We are conspirators in the divine plan of transformation when we choose God and choose one another over and over again, forgiving one another until seventy times seven. In more prosaic terms, we are called to be involved with the world and with one another in ways we can scarcely imagine. The technical word for this is incarnation—enfleshment in a particular time and place.

Our time is now. We do not seek to escape history. I believe we are called to nothing less than the reimagining of Christianity, reentering the tradition in such a way that we begin to trust the future because the future is God's.

Our risk lies in choosing one another over and over again in the face of failure and disappointment. This is what being in love means. The church is a dangerous place because it calls out the best that is in us—the desire to do the right thing and to be good, not in a superficial, goody-goody way but in the deep sense of being true to who we are in God. It is dangerous because we forget that the derring-do originates with God and that it is beautiful. When we forget that our longing for the good and the true is grounded in the beautiful, the spiritual life degenerates into moralism and perfectionism and a cruel idealism overtakes us, mobilizing our resentments and making us harsh and judgmental. Living in the Spirit, on the other hand, means choosing not to live from our resentments and disappointments but from our new life in Christ. And we have to go on choosing right, up until the end.

The Challenge of the Spirit
Some of us are harder to choose than others! Some church people are professional carpers and criticizers who treat the church as if it were a disappointing supermarket of spiritual entitlements. But we have to go on choosing one another anyway. That's why forgiveness and generosity of spirit are givens. The Spirit is challenging the church with

1. our continually having to choose one another—not once but over and over again,
2. our having generously to renegotiate our partnership with one another over and over again,
3. our constantly leaving "home" and building a more open and hospitable one,
4. and our counting the cost.

What would a community open to the Spirit look like? It would be a eucharistic community (one that gives thanks) and it would be a repentant community, always open to conversion. One way the Spirit works on us is through repentance (saying we're sorry) and compunction (having our hearts punctured and cut to the quick). Repentance and compunction provide the protocols—the saving structures—against abuse and manipulation. The capacity to feel sorry for what we have done and the grace to admit it provide the public debate with the lucidity to go forward. When we truly repent, we enter a larger world of new possibilities. We understand that community is not an end in itself but a by-product, which stretches us beyond our limits, of a vision of what human beings are. The work of the Spirit is to unsettle us through love. We don't build community by building community. We build it by having our eye on something else. What is that "something else"? God in Christ. God's great risk is manifested, for example, in the eucharistic table. A eucharistic community is humbled and amazed by the humility of God who is available to us in such simplicity. The Spirit is also practical, pushing issues at us in the democratic experiment, in the confusion and challenge of everyday life. A democratic society requires citizens who can repent—admit their mistakes and not gloss over their shameful acts. A democratic society needs citizens who are committed to telling the truth even if they seldom get it quite right. It is our seldom "getting it right" that necessitates the ongoing conversation and our ongoing conversion. John Gardner writes: "The play of conflicting interests in a framework of shared purposes is the drama of a free society. It is a robust exercise and a noisy one, not for the faint-hearted or the tidy-minded. Diversity is not simply 'good' in that it implies breadth of tolerance and sympathy. A community of diverse elements has greater capacity to adapt and renew itself in a swiftly changing world."[54] In short, the Spirit calls us to be a compassionate and critical community with clear values. The Spirit demands of us a strenuous form of spiritual maturity as we gather round one table.

Imagining a Spirit-Filled Future
What if we live into the challenges the Spirit lays before us? What if we're caught up in the boundless reality of God, transforming simple belief into a journey into God's mystery? What if we cast aside a flattening literalism to discover that poetry and imagination are the pathways of faith? We lose nothing and stand to gain something amazing. We just might come to see that all the great doctrines don't have to be rejected but can return to us as metaphors and stories that aren't really arbitrary after all—they point to and celebrate something real.

And religion, lived out in real life, is a funny thing. You can have two people saying the same words but the meanings and interpretations are at odds. Two people may say the same prayers, repeat the same creeds, even sit in the same pew at the same church. But their hearts—and their religion—may be very different indeed. One is full of love and the other is gripped by a repellent obsessiveness. That's because the *way* we hold our beliefs is as important as the beliefs themselves. I've met people who are fanatical about literal belief in the resurrection, but whose lack of love and compassion empties the belief of all content. Of course, the fact that some people are fanatical doesn't invalidate the truth of the doctrine. Wicked and stupid people can say true things. But when it comes to matters of faith, there has to be some cash value—beliefs should make a difference in the way we behave and think.

Our beliefs surely ought to make a difference in the way we treat one another. But consider the acrimonious and bitter conflicts among the various camps of Anglicans today. There's a celebrated couplet by William Blake in his poem "The Everlasting Gospel," quoted by Rowan Williams, that sums up for me much that is disturbing about some Anglican versions of Christianity.

> That vision of Christ which thou dost see
> Is my vision's greatest enemy.[55]

The archbishop writes, "People who say to one another, 'If you think *that*, you shouldn't be here,' are . . . implicitly echoing Blake's horrifying couplet." And he goes on, "But what gives conflicts their bitterness? What makes them cut us to the bone so that we bleed and suffer? What gives them their resilience and permanence, their power to cloud our thoughts and prayers for weeks on end?"[56] It is a terrible thing to hate and fear someone else's vision of the thing we love most—whether it be Christ, North America, or even our way of life. We attack one another with amazing ferocity around the things we love most. Columnist George Will wrote: "America is currently awash in an unpleasant surplus of clanging, clashing certitudes. That is why there is a rhetorical bitterness absurdly disproportionate to our real differences. It has been well said that the spirit of liberty is the spirit of not being too sure that you are right. One way to immunize ourselves against misplaced certitude is to contemplate—even to savor—the unfathomable strangeness of everything, including ourselves."[57] Spirit, the archbishop says, is "that which realizes, in the endless diversity of human lives, the set of renewed human possibilities opened up by the work of Christ."[58] In a world apparently mesmerized by a fragmenting nihilism, living in the Spirit is the way of our resisting the terrible violence that rips apart our common life. Our faith teaches us how to face death "in the sober letting-go of our fantasies in the sure hope that a faithful God holds us firmly in life and death alike. This is the hope that allows us to recognize power for what it is and isn't: As what is given us for the setting-free of each other, not as the satisfying of our passion for control."[59]

I wonder why we're at each other's throats? At least, it seems that way. Maybe it's because so many of us feel powerless and victimized. We live in a time when we all like to claim victim status (which does disservice to real victims). Even the perpetrator of violence manages to reverse reality to see himself as "victim." The Nazis persuaded themselves that the Jews were "vermin," which needed to be exterminated. Our tendency is to see ourselves as victims of those we persecute. We long for the imagined purity of the past, and look for someone to blame because that lovely past has been sullied. But the perfect past never existed at all. (The perfect past of, for example, Greater Serbia, for which Bosnian villages were "cleansed," never existed in the first place.) But we still cling to the vision, because it not only comforts, it justifies as well. It justifies our illusion that we are fighting the enemies of truth. We sometimes think that we're combating hate when actually we are creating it. We like to think of ourselves as either sinless or helpless or both. That's why so many claim victim status. Historically, we've moved through various claims to sinlessness. The Marxists did it with "the sinless proletariat." Feminists have given us their version of sinlessness, as have blacks and gays. Now white males are screaming for victim status. It's not that there aren't real victims of injustice but that victimhood is abused in our society, which undermines the cries for justice from real victims. It is a terrible sign that we've given up on each other. When we give up on the conversation or when we simply opt out or go to sleep, the world tends to move toward totalitarian solutions.

Religion seems to be showing more and more of its ugly side. I hesitate to use the word "fascist" to describe this trend. It can often be a cheap shot at anyone with whom we disagree. Fascism starts with grievances taking root and then establishing a power base. Lewis Lapham, in his October 2005 editorial in *Harper's Magazine*, cites Umberto Eco's 1995 essay in *The New York Review of Books* on the shape of the fascist mentality. I was struck by his description of a way of thinking or habit of mind that seems very much alive today. Things like:

1. The truth is revealed once and only once;
2. Doctrine outpoints reason, and science is always suspect;
3. Critical thought is the province of degenerate intellectuals, who betray the culture and subvert traditional values;
4. The national identity is provided by the nation's enemies;
5. Argument is tantamount to treason.

Lapham is biting in his criticism. He thinks we're well on the way to a kind of fascism. After all, we don't have to burn any books (as the Nazis did).

We can count it as a blessing that we don't bear the burden of an educated citizenry. The systematic destruction of the public school and library systems over the last thirty years, a program wisely carried out under administrations both Republican and Democratic, protects the market for the sale and distribution of the government's propaganda posters. The publishing companies can print as many books as will guarantee their profit (books on any and all subjects, some of them even truthful), but to people who don't know how to read or think, they do as little harm as snowflakes falling on a frozen pond.[60]

He ends his article with bitter sarcasm: with our trade deficit and national debt, "to say nothing of expanding the markets for global terrorism—I think we can look forward with confidence to character-building bankruptcies, picturesque bread riots, thrilling cavalcades of splendidly costumed motorcycle police." [61]

Fascist movements thrive on insecurity and we are insecure. And it hits close to home when people not only of the same religion but of the same tradition cannot speak to one another, judge one another without a hearing, and anathematize one another on hearsay or selective quotation.

INTERLUDE

Read this story from the Jewish mystical tradition. It sets the tone for our search for a credible and compassionate orthodoxy.

In the beginning before there were any beginnings and endings, there was no place that was not already God! And we call this unimaginable openness, *Ain Soph*—Being–without end. Then came the urge to give life to our world and to us. But there was no place that was not already God. So *Ain Soph* breathed in to make room, like a father steps back so his child will walk to him. Into the emptiness *Ain Soph* set vessels and began to fill them with divine light, as a mother places bowls in which to pour her delicious soup. As the light poured forth a perfect world was being created!

Think of it! A world without greed and cruelty and violence! But then, something happened. The bowls shattered. No one knows why. Perhaps the bowls were too frail? Perhaps the light too intense? Perhaps *Ain Soph* was learning. After all no one makes perfect the first time. And with the shattering of the bowls, divine sparks threw everywhere! Some rushing back to *Ain Soph*, some falling, falling, trapped in the broken shards to become our world, and us.

Though this is hard to believe, the perfect world is all around us, but broken into jagged pieces, like a puzzle thrown to the floor, the picture lost, each piece without meaning, until someone puts them back together again. We are that someone. There is no one else. We are the ones who can find the broken pieces, remember how they fit together and rejoin them. This is the repairing of the world—the mending of creation. In every moment, with every act, we can heal our world and us. We are all holy sparks dulled by separation.

But when we meet, and talk and eat and make love, when we work and play and disagree with holiness in our eyes, seeing *Ain Soph* everywhere, then our brokenness will end, and our bowls will be strong

41

enough to hold the light, and our light will be gentle enough to fill the bowls. As we repair the world together, we will learn that there is no place that is not God!

When we meet, and talk and eat and make love, when we work and play and disagree with holiness in our eyes, seeing *Ain Soph* everywhere, then our brokenness will end. And the conversation can begin.

PART II

The Anglican Conversation:
Caricatures of Anglicanism and Its Discontents

PART II

The Anglican Conversation:
Caricatures of Anglicanism and Its Discontents

There is something unsaid under any given society . . . There's a
symptom apparent in America right now. It's evident in political talk
shows, in entertainment coverage, in artistic criticism of every
kind, in religious discussion. We are living in a courtroom culture . . .
in a culture of extreme advocacy, of confrontation, of judgment, of
verdict . . . Public talking has become obnoxious and insincere.
—John Patrick Shanley, in his introduction to his play, *Doubt*[62]

There was an old statement about being an Anglican, both affectionate and sarcastic, that was going around when I was growing up in England: "The great thing about being an Anglican is that it doesn't interfere with your politics or your religion." Richard Holloway, the former primus of the Church of Scotland, captures something of the affectionate side when he writes:

> The Anglican church is a tolerant, faintly detached and amused mother of lazily permissive standards, but she is a real mother, nevertheless. She does not hector or bully her children. She expects them to be mature and independent. There are certain house rules she likes observed in her home, a sort of minimal but important standard, but if her children break it she doesn't go into an operatic tantrum. She merely raises her eyebrows and wishes they had better manners. Anglicans are not persecutors or excommunicators. We tend to agree with Montaigne, that it is rating our conjectures too highly to roast people alive for them.[63]

This was written over twenty years ago and it seems that much of that

45

easygoing tolerance has gone out the window. Holloway, in 1983, strikes a warning note about the kind of zeal and idealism that does real harm in the name of truth and goodness. He wrote, "We should care for consequences as well as purity of thought. Maybe we should be much humbler about the claims we make, the opinions we push. Come to think of it, maybe we should just gather our lanterns and follow dear Keble through the snow to say the Litany for the Church 'in its present distress.'"[64]

Call Anglicans fuzzy and vague if you must. But not about the things that really matter. For me, some things are completely unambiguous: I believe we can recover the *via media* as the *via regia*—the middle way as the royal way—of Christian commitment. I believe there is a critical mass of Anglicans in general—and Episcopalians in particular—who have a passion for moderation. I believe in Anglican orthodoxy—a rule of faith that guides our path, especially now.

The Anglican Communion is in great distress not least because so many of its members have forgotten the Anglican Way. Can we recover the *via media* as the *via regia* of Christian commitment? Is there a critical mass of Anglicans in general and Episcopalians in particular who have a passion for moderation? Recent converts to Roman Catholicism from Anglicanism think Anglican comprehensiveness is an illusion, a sham, a chimera—a kind of ecclesiastical Camelot.[65] It is thought that there is no such a thing as Anglican orthodoxy—a rule of faith to guide our path. I beg to differ. Anglicanism is still the one tradition that enables me to call myself a Christian. We are not fuzzy and vague about the things that matter. And as for that imaginary Camelot, it seems closer to Rome than to Canterbury.

Caricature One: We're Fuzzy

The first and probably most popular Anglican caricature goes like this: Anglicans stand for nothing in particular. And those who sketch the caricatures belong to two distinct schools. On the one side are the secularists—those cultured despisers of Christianity—and on the other, the dogmatists, who find our reluctance to be pinned down both pathetic and treacherous. Both sides find us funny at best, contemptuous at worst. On the religious side are the champions of a partisan orthodoxy of the left and right who believe that the gospel is betrayed by moderation, by listening, by moving slowly, by an openness to opposing views. They have a point. But it annoys them when I admit it. If they have a point, they demand, why don't I go along with it? Things have got so bad, they seem to say, that the only way forward is to take sides and set up the barricades. "For God's sake," they insist, "stand for *something!*"

My friend Rabbi Stephen Pearce tells the story of the couple, marriage falling apart, who go to their rabbi for counsel. First the woman pours out all her grievances as her husband glumly listens. When she is finished, the rabbi looks at her intently and says, "You're right." Now it's the husband's turn. After his tale of woe, the rabbi looks intently at him and says, "You're right." The wife is furious. "How can you say that to him? How can we both be right?" The rabbi looks at her and says, "You know, you're right!" There must be something Jewish about Anglicanism! We are able to see all sides of an argument.

Bertrand Russell accused his fellow philosopher Alfred North Whitehead of being muddleheaded. Whitehead countered that Russell was simpleminded. Whitehead was an Anglican and Russell an atheist-Puritan. Paul G. Kuntz insists that they need to be in conversation with each other. Both have their tragic aspects. "Russell wants above all to foresee a brighter future for human kind. But he was cast historically in the role of Cassandra. . . . Similarly, Whitehead's philosophy of creative order has to face the entropic loss of all orders except randomness." And Kuntz asks a question of philosophy that can be asked even more intensely of religion: "If we fall apart ideologically into right and left or whatever other polarization makes us cleave to one and hate the other, is there no philosophic center to hold opposites together?"[66] Anglicans at their best do just that. It does not mean that we are without convictions. We affirm that anyone devoted to the discovery of truth needs to maintain "a sense of humor about the wisdom for fighting for victory or negotiating a peace." Being right is important but there may, on occasion, be more important things than being right.

That ability to hold opposites together has any number of practical applications for the church. One church I visited recently had a banner inside that proclaimed, "We are a pro-choice Church." I am deeply repelled by that, not because I am against choice but because it excludes people—like me—for whom this issue is not only painful but also complicated. I am pro-choice but I am not happy about it. I want to leave room in the church for argument and conversation about all the issues about the sanctity of life that the question of choice raises. But we seem to have embraced a theology powered by resentful and toxic certainty. As Nelson Mandela said, "Resentment is like drinking poison and then hoping it will kill your enemies."

When I'm not careful, I can fall into the same trap. So I try—for Christ's sake—to be an "inverse paranoid"—the opposite of a paranoid—and do my best to assume that everyone is part of a plot to enhance my well-being. I try not to be resentful about others being resentful. I have a *passion* for moderation.

Caricature Two: We're Lukewarm
Another Anglican caricature, one of the most recent efforts from the secular side, is by Matthew Parris writing in the *Spectator* in an article entitled "Why the Church of England Is Our Best Defense against Religious Enthusiasm."

The Established Church . . . understood in her bones two great truths: the English are wary about religion; but the English do not want to be atheists. To the English mind, atheism itself carries an unpleasant whiff of enthusiasm. To the English mind, the universe is a very mysterious thing and should be allowed to remain so. And so the English church became what up to our own day it has always remained: a God-fearing receptacle for intelligent doubt; the marrying of a quietist belief in order, duty, decency and the evident difference between right and wrong with a shrewd suspicion that anyone who thinks he can be sure of more than that is probably dangerous. . . . That right at the center of [English] national life, should have stood for so long this great and lovely edifice of sort-of-religion, adorned (through her buildings, her rituals, her art and her music) with so much beauty, so much grace and so much balm for troubled spirits, and served in her priesthood by so many luminously decent men, has surely for centuries helped confound atheism on the one hand, and serious religious enthusiasm on the other. Not so much religious belief as religious relief, this has calmed everybody down. "You really don't need to decide," has been Anglicanism's refrain," and besides, who knows?[67]

There is, of course, a kernel of truth in the tongue-in-cheek description of our tradition. As we have seen, Anglican orthodoxy begins and ends with mystery. Walker Percy, in his novel *The Second Coming*, has his protagonist ask, "Do you realize what it's like to live in the middle of twelve million fundamentalists? The nice thing about Episcopalians is that you'd never mistake them for Christians!"[68] A compliment and an insult at the same time. But the criticism that we are so open-minded that we are empty-headed is unfair. We have our doubts but we don't wallow in them. We appreciate ambiguity but don't make it into a virtue.

More Caricatures
Other caricatures are more probing. Theater director Peter Brook wrote this nearly forty years ago about the then-new cathedral in Coventry, England. It was built

according to the best recipe for achieving a noble result. Honest, sincere artists, the 'best', have been grouped together to make a civilized stab at celebrating God and Man and Culture and Life through a collective act. So there is a new building, fine ideas, beautiful glasswork—only the ritual is threadbare. Those Ancient and Modern hymns, charming perhaps in a little country church, those numbers on the wall, those dog-collars and lessons—they are sadly inadequate here. The new place cries out for a new ceremony, but of course it is the new ceremony that should have come first—it is the ceremony in all its meanings that should have dictated the shape of the place, as it did when all the great mosques and cathedrals and temples were built. Goodwill, sincerity, reverence, belief in culture are not quite enough: then outer form can only take on real authority if the ceremony has equal authority—and who today can possibly call the tune? . . . We have lost all sense of ritual and ceremony . . . but the words remain with us and old impulses stir in the marrow. . . . It is not the fault of the holy that it has become a middle-class weapon to keep children good.[69]

There's some truth in this—and even some prophecy. Where many of the liberals got it wrong has been precisely in the area of ritual. The Latin Mass is on the way back. There are signs that the young, while still wanting to think for themselves, long for mystery and the transcendent in liturgy and find the offerings thin and threadbare. Rationalism is never enough.

The old Anglicanism of my parents and grandparents has been described unfairly as "a kind of domesticated pantheism: a communion with shrubberies and rockeries, the song thrush at the bird bath, with the look in the eye of a reliably well-behaved dog."[70] Now England is seen as post-Christian and postimperial, where a religion shaped for a very English God is showing signs of strain now that England has nothing outside itself to rule and conquer. And the cheapest caricature of our agnosticism is this: "What friends call honest doubt, or seeking, enemies call hypocrisy. Many Anglicans, content to rub shoulders with God will say and sing words they are light-years from believing."[71]

Beyond the Caricatures

But the internal critics of Anglicanism—those who love it and are hurt and disappointed—deserve more attention than those who caricature us. It is fair to ask, "Are we becoming casual drifters with no roots? Is this where the secular project has brought us?" The conservatives have a point. As the "liberal" and always interesting and provocative theologian Don Cupitt writes, people are becoming "de-traditionalized, nomadized, casualized." In the brave new world we find,

> instead of marriage, a series of relationships; instead of a home, a series of addresses; instead of a career, freelancing; instead of a church, the irregularly mushrooming politics of protest; instead of a faith, whatever one is currently "into"; instead of stable identities, pluralism and flux; instead of society, the market and one's own circle. These are times when the intellectual climate is very permissive, as if . . . the culture has suddenly become all fringe and no mainstream.[72]

There's bound to be a reaction. As the old fixed points of reference disappear, we become frightened and look for tradition and find rigidity; we look for stability and opt for slavery; we ache to be grounded and find ourselves in prison. Our imagination is presented with terrible choices: dogmatic traditionalism or materialistic consumerism—which ends in screamingly boring secularism or merely profitable corruption. *But the Anglican Tradition as I have received it insists that there is hope because these are not the only choices.*

Back to the Future

Which brings us back to the old question: Are we in the middle of a new Dark Ages? It's dangerous to draw historical parallels, but old ways of running the world are breaking down, as they did at the fall of the Roman Empire. "What did people do then, when the world was falling apart?" Alasdair McIntyre wondered. What they did, he wrote, was to look—perhaps quite unconsciously—for *new forms of community* "within which the moral life could be sustained so that both morality and civility might survive the coming age of barbarism and darkness."[73] Have we also not reached a turning point? McIntyre goes on, "This time however the barbarians are not waiting beyond the frontiers; they have already been governing us for quite some time." I think that's where some of us are—looking for new forms of community—looking for a new St. Benedict.

The trouble is that communities formed in a world falling apart yearn for strict rules for membership and clear criteria for excommunication. Sometimes we notice this and sometimes we don't. We can easily spot the ways we exclude based on race and gender, but not where it comes to political opinions. The new Christian Right, for example, is a crusade to change American society with highly specific programs, about which there is no shadow of doubt. The same can be said of some left-wing believers. Both the left and the right suffer from the disease of God-is-on-our-side-ism. Peter Berger pointed this out years ago with relish. "God is *for* tuition tax credits; God is against them. God is for the MX missile; God is against it. God is pro-life; God is pro-choice." We stand in two places at once. With regard to our religious or political affiliations we feel stuck between what Berger calls "thugs and wimps . . . the Rambos on one side and the Mary Poppinses on the other."[74] This tendency can play a part in the way our future takes shape. Our future looks back to ancient Rome in another way. Tom Cahill has his own hopeful vision of the new coming truly "catholic" and "orthodox" community. At the end of his *How the Irish Saved Civilization*, he suggests that the affluent and powerful are the Romans of the twentieth century; our communications system is the modern-day equivalent of the Roman roads. But he warns that

that road system became impassable rubble, as the empire was overwhelmed by population explosions beyond its borders. So will ours. Rome's demise instructs us in what inevitably happens when impoverished and rapidly expanding populations, whose ways and values are only dimly understood, press up against a rich and ordered society. More than a billion people in our world today survive on less than $370 a year, while Americans, who constitute five percent of the world's population, purchase fifty percent of its cocaine. If the world's population, which has doubled in our lifetime, doubles again by the middle of the next century, how could anyone hope to escape the catastrophic consequences—the wrath to come? But we turn our backs on such unpleasantness and contemplate the happier prospects of our technological dreams.

What will be lost and what will be saved of our civilization probably lies beyond our powers to decide. No human group has ever figured out how to design its future. That future may be germinating today not in a boardroom in London or an office in Washington or a bank in Tokyo, but in some antic outpost or other—a kindly British orphanage in the grim foothills of Peru, a house for the dying in a back street of Calcutta run by a fiercely single-minded Albanian nun, an easygoing French medical team at the starving edge of the Sahel, a mission to Somalia by Irish social workers who remember their own Great Hunger, a nursery program to assist convict-mothers at a New York prison—in some unheralded corner where a great-hearted human being is committed to loving in an extraordinary way.

Perhaps history is always divided into Romans and Catholics—or, better, catholics. The Romans are the rich and powerful who run things their way and must always accrue more because they instinctively believe that there will never be enough to go around; the catholics, as their name implies, are universalists who instinctively believe that all humanity makes one family, that every human being is an equal child of God, and that God will provide. "The twenty-first century," prophesied Malraux, "will be spiritual or it will not be."[75]

Which Orthodoxy Is Orthodox? Struggling with the Conversation

There are many rival orthodoxies with their clear rules for excommunication. Each side tells the stories to suit their clientele. On left or right, there are no ambiguities, no areas of uncertainty. You can smell the anger and despair in the air when people feel that there is no community of trust, no saving word binding them together, no God worth believing in, no tale to tell. Perhaps it's our lack of consciousness of this anger and despair that constitutes part of our predicament. As McIntyre predicted, we seem to be waiting for another—doubtless very different—St. Benedict—a strong and confident voice like that of the sixth-century monk, who offered not only a vision of community but an actual expression of it in a world that was crumbling.

Orthodoxy, to have any value, means belonging to a community of trust and authority. But how do we build a community of trust from disparate and contradictory elements? *How* we deal with our resentments and disappointments will determine the kind of community we are building. Communities of resentment and hate are alive and well. We long for St. Benedict's ordered freedom. But that can only happen in a community marked by obedience— not only to an abbot but to one another. Obedience means listening and, sadly, we don't listen. And the commitment to listen to one another is a central virtue in Christian community.

With so many disparate voices within the church, sometimes it's really hard to listen. Conservative critics within the church rightly raise the issue of the limits of pluralism and point to the absurdity of so insisting on "diversity" that the result is fragmentation. What to others may seem fuzzy and vague to us is a matter of reverence before mystery. At certain moments and at our best, we are willing to say, "We don't know. We'll have to think about that." The collection of Rowan Williams's essays, *On Christian Theology*,[76] addresses our anxiety about being no longer sure what Christianity is about. He asks disturbing questions about, for example, the danger of privatizing the moral imagination, which, with its emphasis on the person rather than on the community, would only help us avoid the pressing issues facing the human family: environmental degradation, women's rights, and the fate of the world's children. The archbishop dares to ask something one couldn't imagine a fundamentalist asking, "Has not a redemption-oriented Christian theology functioned as an expression of the male urge to shake off the threatening and humiliating ties that bind spirit to body, to the earth, to the cycle of reproduction, woman imaged as the sign of fallenness, of unspiritual nature?"[77]

Problems with Liberal and Conservative Orthodoxy

One of the heresies of some "conservative" interpretations of Christianity is the idea that the gospel means the liberation of spirit from nature and, we might add, history. Hence Williams (following Rosemary Ruether's *Sexism and God-Talk: Toward a Feminist Theology*, 1983) identifies two problems for twenty-first century Christians: dualism and hierarchy—the split between spirit and matter and the abuse of power. These are issues that conservatives, on the whole, do not want to talk about.

But there are issues the liberals shy away from too. Liberals, in general, don't like to talk about the limits of pluralism. But pluralism can become a

"repressive tolerance"; "an intellectually idle and morally frivolous prohibi-
tion against raising uncomfortable questions about Christian truth."[78]
Liberals don't want to face the sillinesses of much of multiculturalism, which
claims that all cultural practices are to be tolerated and valued. Even the most
thoughtless are brought up short by a subject like the practice of female cir-
cumcision. Maybe not all cultural practices are desirable and to be respect-
ed? When either side shies away from issues, the conversation either stops or
becomes distorted.

Williams, while insisting that there is a common hope and a common
vocation for human beings, points out that the problem in a radically pluralistic society is that citizens increasingly withdraw from judgment. "The social
system overall sees its job as securing a pragmatic minimum of peaceful coexistence between groups, by a variety of managerial skills and economic
adjustments."[79] There are, in effect, no common values. Things are flattened
out—the neutralizing of genuine political dissent, the system of palliative
welfare benefits, the reduction of the franchise to an almost passive formali-
ty. "Societies that are able to control their populations in such ways do not
need the legitimization of 'values'; they do not need myth or religion or
morality." We are managed. There is no conversation because there is nothing to discuss. It is settled. Style is everything. Cultural options presented as
consumer goods. "Religious belief is no exception . . . religious commitment
is reduced to a private matter of style, unconnected with the nature of a person's membership in his or her society." Our abiding nostalgia for "values"
becomes just window dressing. Conservatives rightly rail at the twin dangers
of a consumer pluralism and the administered and managed society.

One of the recent critics of liberalism in the church is theologian and
Episcopal priest Philip Turner. His article, "An Unworkable Theology" in
First Things (a journal that seems to delight in denigrating all things
Anglican), takes the Episcopal Church to task because of its mania to include
everyone.[80] After reading the article, I spent a depressing hour surfing the
Internet for responses to it, to see if there were any real conversations going on.
All I found were "blog" endorsements by the self-appointed "orthodox"—all
very depressing because the issues are important and deserve true debate.
Turner writes of the Episcopal sermon that

> at its most fulsome, begins with a statement to the effect that the incar-
> nation is merely a manifestation of divine love. From this starting
> point, several conclusions are drawn. The first is that God is love pure
> and simple. Thus one is to see in Christ's death no judgment upon the
> human condition. Rather, one is to see an affirmation of creation and
> the persons we are. The life and death of Jesus reveal the fact that God
> accepts and affirms us.[81]

This vapid theology, he claims, is the prevailing one in the Episcopal Church. "It's a theological chasm—one that separates those who hold a theology of divine acceptance from those who hold a theology of redemption."[82]

That Turner seems to be giving comfort to those who think they have their theology right but are contemptuous of others saddened me. Is that what we've come to? Will this kind of polemic characterize the foreseeable future? Are there no other choices but the unworkable theology he describes so well and the "workable" theology of imagined orthodoxy? (Just take a look at the history of "orthodoxy" and count the bodies.) I was brought up on a fierce "theology of redemption," and in my experience it did great harm. Just as he is unimpressed by the "God is Love" school of preaching, so I am critical of a theology of redemption that is equally unworkable. Surely our faith is stretched and tested by a history of Christianity that is, in one sense, a catalog of failure?

The maddening thing is that Turner is mostly right. He begins with the correct assertion that radical *unqualified* inclusion is a shallow and vapid reduction of the gospel. But he says nothing about the opposite problem of ahistorical and idealist orthodoxy. He bewails the fact that the vapid liberalizing doesn't lead to amendment of life or the pursuit of the holy. But an "orthodoxy" that just means saying the right words doesn't produce holiness of life either. After all, we can say true things falsely.

Turner's accusations hit home. The "liberal" view of Christianity is unappealing and unsatisfactory because it is based on a thin and false anthropology of the isolated autonomous self—of the self pleasing itself in isolation from the community and our obligations to it. Here Turner and I are in agreement. My quarrel with him is not that there is no revelation but that the revelation is of something ultimately mysterious and that we'd better listen to one another to discern what God is trying to tell us. It appears that he thinks I and those like me claim too little (our agnosticism, he contends, is unwarranted) and, from my perspective, his is a counsel of despair.

He characterizes the liberal creed as sentimental interpretation of statements at the heart of the gospel: "God is love. God loves us. We, therefore, ought to love one another." Why be contemptuous of that? It isn't a bad place to start. Indeed, for John of the Cross, it's also the place we should come to at the end. Does Turner really mean to give the impression that he finds the new commandment—to love one another—ludicrous? His thin argument goes like this: Liberals have a shallow view of God's love because there is neither cost nor judgment implicit in that love. There is no call, he says, to amendment of life. I share his irritation at the silly political correctness of radical inclusion—an inclusion that is based on no discernible theological principle. But why ridicule people's passion for social justice? In classic

Christian theology there are two kinds of inclusion or solidarity: solidarity in sin and solidarity in glory. The human family is one in its fallenness and also one in its longing for glory. Thus, "inclusion" certainly calls for repentance and amendment of life.

Does the gospel of the kingdom, then, have nothing to say about inclusion, hospitality, and social justice—all words that Turner seems to despise? Is there a *necessary* chasm between the theologies of acceptance and redemption? Couldn't the latter express the cost of the former? Why does "radical hospitality" get up his nose? Where does he get the idea that those who disagree with him aren't interested in repentance and amendment of life? My sadness comes from the fact that we could so easily make common cause.

Basic Questions

The underlying question, of course, is the one of authority and discipline. Here we seem to be in agreement. I feel less and less at home in the Episcopal Church and yet have a great regard for my formative time in England, where I was touched for good by both the evangelical and catholic wings of our tradition. I feel a deep connection to Chartres cathedral and find myself looking to an increasingly Anglican-looking Roman Catholicism. Roman Catholicism isn't as coherent as the Vatican would have us believe. So I envy the fact that Turner has found a home—but it isn't one that beckons me. Why does a generosity of spirit (and leaving the judging to God) reduce the significance of Christ's resurrection and downplay holiness of life as a fundamental marker of Christian identity? Why does it *necessarily* undermine the Trinitarian vision? Of course, there are many smug and silly liberals, but smugness and silliness aren't the exclusive characteristics of liberals.

The tragedy is that while much of Turner's diagnosis is correct, his inferences are not. His conclusions are not only way off the mark but, in spirit, deeply unfair. Surely there are liberal and conservative Episcopalians who know their need for a Savior, their need for forgiveness and healing. Surely they, like Turner and Jones, stumble in responding to the call to conversion and radical holiness. Don't we all share an anguish about the general failure of Christianity through the ages? Many of us don't know where to turn. So we look for certainties in the theologies of the *Left Behind* series, of reactionary Roman Catholicism, of African Anglicanism—all of them as deeply flawed as the flabby liberalism that believes God loves everyone.

I agree completely with Turner's statement about "'Nicene Christianity,' with its thick description of God as Father, Son, and Holy Spirit, its richly developed Christology, and its compelling account of Christ's call to holiness of life." Yes! But let's be in conversation. It's my experience—as a priest and confessor—that people find it almost impossible to believe that they are loved, really loved. And there's nothing easy or sentimental about that.

In this regard, Rowan Williams writes of the Abbé Huvelin—a great nine-teenth-century spiritual director who suffered from ill health and deep depression. He also endured gout and migraine, and the thought of suicide was a current obsession. Huvelin was not a whole man—today we would say that he lacked proper self-love and authentic self-valuing. His sense of his own worthlessness was intense, yet he was able to transmit hope to others. People flocked to him for counsel, and he gave them his attention and com-passion. I take great comfort in the fact that deeply injured and fearful—psy-chologically scarred—people can be agents of love. It means that there is hope for us all.

Rowan Williams points out that the Abbé Huvelin was accessible—he spent most of his time listening to people in a way that suggests he was enlarged, not diminished, by his suffering. Good news. The Abbé Huvelin wrote: "The more you suffer, the more you understand that souls are, above all, beings that suffer, and that they stand in need more of relief and conso-lation than of rebuke and correction."[83]

The more I have presumed to engage in the art of spiritual direction, the more hesitant I am to make moral judgments. A deep tenderness is required because of the tragedy and glory of being human—the mess of it all. I think of the rigid-minded bigot whose humanity was revealed to me when he talked about his son, who was addicted to cocaine. I was touched by a friend of mine, a French Roman Catholic priest who, over thirty years ago, heard confessions at the shrine of St. Thérèse of Lisieux and was told by one of his superiors that his being too lenient with sinners assisted in their perdition. Thank God he had the courage to follow his heart. I think of the late Brother David—a Franciscan friend—who, years ago, reluctantly heard my confes-sion because he was sick of people concentrating too much on their sins and not enough on God's love. Instead of my making a formal confession, we talked for an hour about my life and the messes I'd gotten into, and the mys-tery of God's love. And then at the end, he prayed over me:

O my God, you are here.
O my God, I am here.
O my God, Alan is here.
O my God, we are here.
And always, always, you love us;
When we are good
with a love that makes you glad;
when we are bad
with a love that makes you sad,
but always, always, you love us!

Insofar as I have lived this prayer, I have found it good news, the antidote to the violence in my soul and a means of grace for the peace of the world. I pray that we all get the direction we need when we need it. God is always reaching out to us if we could see. Always, always, God loves us. I can see why an unbeliever would find this sentimental and annoying but puzzled why a believer should. Isn't it orthodox to believe so?

Whether we are liberals or conservatives or something in between, always, always, God loves us. And it is costly.

PART III

The Promise of Anglican Orthodoxy

Part III

The Promise of Anglican Orthodoxy

A saint is someone whose life has been insufficiently researched.
—Anonymous

Every definition is a misfortune.
—Erasmus

Nowadays, I find myself at home in disparate places, with many friends in other traditions. An important one was Albert Lander, the head verger at Grace Cathedral, San Francisco, who became a member of St. Dominic's Roman Catholic Church while staying in full communion with his Anglican friends. When he died—too early, at the age of fifty—he had two requiem masses, filled with the glory and pain of our being "almost" in communion. Albert, however, would have none of that "almost." When he was dying, he asked me to bring him the sacrament and to anoint him.

Albert's death and his manner of going through it was a revelation of the utmost clarity. He knew who he was and where he was going. His dying and death taught both communities what it is to be the church. His life revolved around Grace Cathedral—he loved it and gave himself wholeheartedly to it. He was quintessentially an Anglican—an Episcopalian. Yet we found ourselves—a mixed congregation of Christians—in St. Dominic's Roman Catholic Church for his first requiem mass. What was going on? To tell the truth, Albert was a bit of a trickster. I think he was one of those who are called to anticipate the coming church. He was an eschatological Catholic who believed that the full catholicity of the church has yet to be revealed. He understood that our differences are trivial and minor compared with the great things we have in common. Did Albert die a Roman Catholic? Well—yes, he did. Did he die an Episcopalian? Well—yes, he did. It's as if Albert is

61

saying to us, "If you find this confusing, get over it. Look at the bigger picture of God's love and generosity. I died in Christ." On the other side of death, Albert is pulling our leg. Frankly, I think he did it deliberately.

So there we all were at St. Dominic's, which I regard as my parish church, since it's only two blocks from my home. I love it there. In fact, I have a fantasy that by the time I'm ready to retire, I will be able to join that parish without having to change my allegiance at all. I think Albert would have understood that. Meanwhile, we all endure the pain of impaired communion. Timothy Radcliffe, O.P., the former head of the Dominican Order, writes of seeing everyone of good will as a partner in building God's home with us. I like that image of each of us building a shelter for the other. That's the religion I find at St. Dominic's and at Grace Cathedral. Father Timothy writes:

> This can happen in wonderful and unexpected ways. Our Japanese brother Oshida founded a Christian community in the hill near Mt. Fuji. In the garden he set up a statue of the Buddha, with the child Jesus on his lap. The villagers began to come discreetly during the night to leave offerings. A place was coming to be where people of different faiths could gather and prepare for the Kingdom.[84]

By contrast, a few years ago, I spoke at the annual clergy conference of a diocese in the Church of England. In many ways, I felt very much at home, but in others, I felt I was visiting another planet. In a country where people aren't exactly flocking to church, this handful of Anglicans was fragmented. The Anglo-Catholics wouldn't receive communion from their own bishop (a loving man trying to hold this unruly crowd together) because he'd ordained women. A bishop "flew in" and said a bizarre 1662 "High Mass" for them, while the women cried or in anger celebrated their own liturgy. The Evangelicals were beating up on Rowan Williams for being soft on homosexuality, and they got mad at me, too, when I carelessly mentioned "the morally repellent doctrine of penal substitution." I should have been more sensitive to those who believe that the attitude of a just God toward sinners can only be one of wrath and the sinless Jesus appeases the divine anger. In that contentious atmosphere, I found myself—an Anglo-Catholic—more at home with the other two speakers—lovely, generous, articulate men, one a Methodist, the other a Presbyterian. When I heard them speak, I recognized the church I belonged to. I experience the same thing when I hear or read, for example, the Dominican Timothy Radcliffe and the Roman Catholic historian Eamon Duffy—and when I think of Albert and his two requiem masses. The coming church is alive and well—always in the process of reforming itself.

The Heart of Orthodox Anglicanism

One of the most original exponents of the generous vision of Christianity at the heart of orthodox Anglicanism—a Christianity that is loving, mystical, and inclusive—is the late Father Bede Griffiths, former Anglican, tutored by C. S. Lewis at Oxford, who became a Roman Catholic Benedictine and ended his life in 1993 as a holy man in the Hindu tradition in South India. I choose him deliberately because, as an Anglican who became a Roman Catholic Benedictine, he never lost the spirit of his first love.

One of his better-known books is *The Golden String*.[85] His vision of the coming Christianity was indeed loving, mystical, and inclusive. He became a Roman Catholic and entered the Benedictines, and was ordained a priest in 1940. But at the age of fifty, his life changed radically when, visiting India and staying in ashrams, he began to find the other half of his soul. The Jesuit author William Johnston writes, "Griffiths brought English caution, Catholic vision, and Hindu philosophy in conjunction."[86] From about the age of forty on, Griffiths saw what his life was about and committed himself to this mystical vision with an attitude of surrender and observation. In his fifties, he joined the tradition of a sannyasi (monk) and wore the Kavi orange robes. In 1968, he assumed leadership of the Saccidananda, a Christian ashram founded by Henri Le Saux and French priest Jules Monchanin.

What are the marks of Bede Griffiths' orthodoxy that resonate with what I have received from the Anglican tradition? The first and most important is the ability to see God in everyone. The second is the conviction that "the surrender of the ego is the only way of life" and that "it's the most difficult thing we have to do."

In 1990, Griffiths had his first stroke, accompanied by a struggle and "conversion"—"a struggle with death and divine love." This stroke had three levels of influence on him—on his body, soul, and spirit. It helped him overcome dualism to reach a unity assuring him that his body and soul were no longer two. It also led to the awakening, he said, of his suppressed feminine side, which demanded attention and integration. Then, a month after the stroke, he had an intense experience of love. He wept and couldn't speak for several days.

He pointed to two symbols—the Black Madonna and the Crucified Christ. For him, these were signs of the centrality of the divine feminine and the mystery of suffering. The Black Madonna for him was intimately connected with earth mother images—with rocks and caves and nature. "The Black Madonna symbolizes for me the Black Power in Nature and Life, the hidden power in the womb . . . I feel it was this power which struck me. She is cruel and destructive, but also deeply loving and nourishing." And later he wrote, "The figure of the Black Madonna stood for the feminine in all its forms. I felt the need to surrender to the Mother, and this gave me the experience of being overwhelmed by love. I realized that surrendering to death, and dying to oneself is surrendering to Total Love."

About the Crucified Christ, he wrote,

> On the Cross Jesus surrendered himself to this Dark Power. He lost everything: friends, disciples, his own people, their law and religion. And at the last he had to surrender to his God: 'My God, my God, why have you forsaken me?' Even his heavenly Father, every image of a personal God, had to go. He had to enter the Dark Night, to be exposed to the abyss. Only then could he become everything and nothing, opened beyond everything that can be named or spoken; only then could he be one with the darkness, the Void, the Dark Mother who is love itself.

These thoughts are echoed in the words of poet Henry Vaughan (1621–1695): "There be in God, some say, a deep but dazzling darkness"— and in the Eastern Orthodox apophatic tradition. This vision, however, is markedly absent from the kind of "orthodoxy" from which all sense of mystery is absent. Talk of "darkness" and the "feminine" can be very disturbing to those who find their orthodoxy in propositions and verbal correctness. But a commitment to the dazzling darkness of the transcendent yet ever-present God is deeply orthodox. In the darkness we are bound to meet up with things we have repressed and rejected.

Above all, Father Griffiths was a man of prayer. He wrote this about the Jesus Prayer:

> When I say, Lord Jesus, Son of God, I think of Jesus as the Word of God, embracing heaven and earth and revealing himself in different ways and under different names and forms to all humanity. I consider that this Word 'enlightens everyone coming into the world,' and though they may not recognize it, it is present in every human being in the depths of their soul. Beyond word and thought, beyond all signs and symbols, this Word is being secretly spoken in every heart in every place and at every time.

Griffiths believed that we are called to be simply ourselves, and the human adventure is to find that out. Christianity, he believed, is truly about love. His fellow Benedictine, Father Laurence Freeman, was with him soon before he died, and read to him from St. John's Gospel: "This is my commandment that you love one another." Griffiths caught his breath and, lifting his finger in emphasis, said, "That is the whole gospel." Legend has it that the aging John at Ephesus was brought out on a litter from time to time to preach his one and only sermon: God is love. It's this generosity that seems to get up the nose of many who fancy that they are "orthodox." But, as John proclaimed—and as Father Griffiths understood—the love of God is the very heart of orthodoxy.[87]

A Generous Anglican Orthodoxy

In looking for a common language and common purpose—for a generous orthodoxy—we are not looking to found a theocracy or a form of theocratic totalitarianism. We are looking for ways to love one another. Orthodoxy as theocracy assumes that there can be an end to dialogue and discovery. That's why it's so attractive. Believers would have the right to outlaw unbelief, as they have done in the past. Rowan Williams writes, "It assumes that there could be a situation in which believers in effect had nothing to learn . . . the gift of a time of repentance and growth are set aside."

Vladimir Lossky wrote about the work of the Spirit in orthodoxy as "that which realizes in the endless diversity of human lives the set of renewed human possibilities opened up by the work of Christ." Orthodoxy opens horizons. It invites us to a banquet. It does not imprison us in a fortress. A parting word from a retired priest to Archbishop William Levada (off to Rome to be Cardinal Ratzinger's successor) was very encouraging: "Your job is to tell the world how joyful the Gospel is!" I hope so.

The trouble is that "orthodoxy" is a moving target. The "orthodox" point of view of one era is "heterodox" in another. In 1829, Pope Leo XII said that "whoever allows himself to be vaccinated ceases to be a child of God. Smallpox is a judgment of God; the vaccination is a challenge toward heaven." The pope argued that vaccination was an inappropriate interference with the will of God. So, there are things we now take for granted as heterodox (like vaccination) that were once called intrinsically evil and against nature. Slavery, subjugation of women, the refusal to recognize trade unions, anesthesia, divorce—all have been grist for the "orthodox" mill. "Orthodoxy" was often used to keep people in their place. The sermon by the Victorian bishop in Isabel Colegate's *The Summer of the Royal Visit* comes to mind. The fictional bishop saw the burgeoning movements of democracy as flying in the face of the way God had ordered the world. His sermon is addressed to the unwashed who blundered into Bath Abbey:

If the future is in your hands—what will you do with it? You proliferate, you breed, without thought of how you are to be fed . . . Power! What would you do with power? Have you prepared yourselves for it by years of education and training and self-discipline? What do you know of the art of administration? Or of art of any kind? How under your sway can our cities fail to spread and deteriorate and become even uglier and more vulgar, our culture be lost to barbarism, our morals be undermined by atheism, our politics be poisoned by demagoguery? Where is the deference, where the due order of hierarchy? Are we all to be drawn down into the vortex of moral chaos and mere animalism, sucked into the spiritual void which calls itself democracy? We have to ask ourselves for what purpose have we been made.[88]

The purpose of this bishop's "orthodoxy," it seems, was to keep people in their place.

John Henry Newman's genius was to see that orthodoxy develops and changes. But how? What are its limits? If the church is a schooling in conversation, then listening to one another in humility should be our highest priority. Humility before the mystery of God's revelation in Christ might make us hesitate to pontificate prematurely about what is legitimate and what isn't. "Orthodoxy," therefore, has a distinctly moral character. It is validated by the way we treat one another. Revelation has a practical purpose—not that we should "know more" but that we should "do better." The test of true knowledge is love. "Of what use is it if I discourse learnedly on the Trinity and lack humility and, therefore, displease the Trinity?" wrote Thomas à Kempis in his *Imitation of Christ*. We are given only enough light to move ahead. We're not told everything we'd like to know. Newman's hymn comes to mind.

> Lead, Kindly Light, amid the encircling gloom
>   Lead Thou me on!
> The night is dark, and I am far from home—
>   Lead Thou me on!
> Keep Thou my feet; I do not ask to see
> The distant scene—one step enough for me.

That's the humility of orthodoxy.

Practical Orthodoxy

Salvation isn't the ultimate reward for believing abstract doctrines. Salvation is experienced through grace as our lives are "converted," and conversion is an ongoing process. Doctrine is practical. It has to do with *practice*, with what the tradition calls "the experimental knowledge of God." The doctrine of the Trinity, for example, isn't just a cerebral exercise for theologians. It has enormous personal, interpersonal, and political implications. As Archbishop Peter Carnley points out, "The doctrine of the Trinity operates as a kind of model for the way we are and how we behave in the Church as a diversity of distinct and distinguishable persons living in the unity of one communion by mutual self-gift."[89] There must be an interplay between doctrine and experience if it is to be valid.

To be truly orthodox, doctrine must have an impact on the moral life. I remember some years ago a man screaming at the philosopher Jacob Needleman that to be a Christian you had to believe in the physical resurrection of Jesus. Needleman took the wind out of the young man's sails and said, "Yes, you do. Now tell me, what does it mean? Tell me what difference it makes!" The young man had nothing to say. An elderly retired priest angrily thundered at me: "Do you believe in the *homoousian?*" (this is the doctrine that Jesus Christ is of the same substance as the Father). I said, "Yes, I do, but the more important question is why don't you love me?" He saw me as a mindless liberal from San Francisco and therefore incapable of affirming orthodox Christology. The doctrine of the incarnation is central to orthodox believing. It emphasizes the goodness of created things. We celebrate the material world, for example, in the Eucharist. The incarnation also challenges our degradation of the environment. This is what we mean (with Newman) when we say that doctrine is regulative rather than speculative. Doctrine should regulate the way we live our lives and not just the way we speculate about God. Christian witness is compromised over and over again because of the gap between our rhetoric and our behavior. The presenting issue about orthodoxy in the church today is sexuality (homosexuality in particular). We seem unable to discuss the "gay" issue sanely.

For example, I am puzzled at Dr. Paul Zahl's certainty about what the Bible says about homosexuality. Zahl, dean of Trinity Episcopal School for Ministry, writes: "In the case of homosexuality, the Bible is just too unanimous. It declares itself in too weighted and powerful a way. It cannot be explained or otherwise interpreted."[90] I admire Dr. Zahl's zeal for the truth and his insisting that we don't dodge the issue, but I wonder how much he understands homosexuality. Are there subjects on which the Bible is of no help? Surely, from the biblical perspective there are no such beings as homosexuals (oriented toward their own sex). Would it not be truer to say that the Bible understands everyone to be heterosexual and condemns those heterosexuals who behave "perversely"? Wouldn't this, at least, be a point of departure for further conversation? Perhaps the Bible is unanimous about some things but not, in reality, on this one. Is there no room for some hesitancy? Isn't the Bible, in some sense, in conflict with itself? Doesn't our task to discern the word of God require our being in communion and hearing all voices?

On the other side, conservatives like to appeal to a clear and idealized past for their construction of orthodoxy. Historical myths distort the past to lend authority to the present, making its contingent arrangements seem to enshrine eternal truths. With regard to the gay issue, the biblical texts presuppose a world in which there is no differentiation between hetero- and homosexuality. But the biblical writers had no concept of a homosexually orient-ed person. There was just undifferentiated heterosexuality. A few texts in the Bible obviously do refer to homosexual behavior, but there is no clue as to the possibility of homosexually oriented persons in long-term committed relationships. Faithless promiscuity is roundly condemned in the Bible, but that doesn't help us in thinking about faithful long-term relationships. The point about the Bible is that the texts trigger discussion. They do not settle the matter.

Changing Orthodoxy

Historical Roman Catholicism is littered with unsettled matters, no matter how vigorously the *magisterium* may deny it. John T. Noonan Jr., one of San Francisco's distinguished Roman Catholics, has written a book, *When Old Certainties Give Way: A Church That Can and Cannot Change*, about how the church has struggled to devote itself to the apostles' teaching on, for exam-ple, slavery and banking (usury), religious freedom, and the indissolubility of marriage. His writing is all the more telling today in the light of the official Roman Catholic Church's unwillingness to admit the possibility of change in its moral teachings.

In 1965, for example, many theologians came to the conclusion that the church's teaching on contraception should change. The church was ready to say so, but Pope Paul VI claimed he could not change the teaching because the church and the hierarchical *magisterium* had taught it for so long. Here's a little history lesson: The late pope never recognized the possibility that papal teaching on moral issues might be wrong. The *magisterium* continues to insist that artificial contraception is *intrinsically evil* and *against nature*—two formulas that seem to deny any possibility of change.

Think of usury—making a profit from a loan. It was once considered intrinsically evil because it went against the "nature" of money. A series of popes taught that it was an evil and so did three general councils of the church, and so did all the bishops. Everywhere and at all times usury, the mak-ing of profit from a loan, was condemned as sin. That was the orthodox point of view. Catholic theologians finally accepted usury at the end of the sixteenth century, but it was not until the eighteenth century that popes did so.

A great doctrine, now a pillar of orthodoxy and in tune with the apostles' teaching, is freedom of conscience. This is something all free societies take for granted. Yet Pope Gregory XVI, following a very long tradition, taught in an 1832 encyclical that *freedom of conscience* in society was "absurd and erro-neous" or rather "folly" (*deliramentum*). Thank God the late pope, John Paul II, taught the opposite. It is now considered to be "intrinsically evil" to coerce rational human beings. So it's sometimes hard to trust the Roman Catholic Church because of its selective amnesia. John Paul II was great at asking the children of the church to repent their errors but did not ask the church itself to do so.

Struggling toward Orthodoxy

The different traditions need each other. The tragedy of Roman Catholicism is its papalization. The tragedy of Anglicanism is its lack of structure. The two traditions need each other. Think of what it felt like to be an Anglican the day after Charles I lost his head in 1649. Think of what it was like for thoughtful Roman Catholics to realize that Pius IX, in 1870, was paranoid about infallibility. In a scary private audience, he berated Cardinal Guidi, the Dominican archbishop of Bologna, as a traitor for suggesting that the pope could make no infallible utterance without first consulting the other bishops. "I *am* the tradition!" he bellowed.[91] And some now want to canonize him!

Historian Eamon Duffy accuses some Roman Catholics of longing for "history without bewilderment or tears." He writes, "There are huge questions . . . about what exactly constitutes the essence of Catholicism, and how, in a world as diverse and pluralistic as ours, the spiritual coherence of Catholicism can be sustained and nourished without intellectual aridity or coercion." The maxim "Error has no rights!" cuts off conversation. "For more than a millennium the Catholic Church thought it right to combat heresy and enforce orthodoxy and Catholic morality by the use of force, including the death penalty." Part of the great work of the Second Vatican Council in 1965 was *The Declaration on Religious Liberty* as a fundamental human right. For many in the church, this was a bombshell. How could fifteen hundred years of church teaching be wrong? The statement wasn't addressing remote problems about the distant past—the Vatican in recent memory had approved the Spanish state's putting its Protestant citizens at a disadvantage.

Pius IX and those Anglicans and Protestants like him who deny debate and plurality might contemplate this statement from Duffy.

Agreement in the great Councils of the Church was not the product of blinding flashes of revelation or the tranquil reiteration of familiar and uncontentious unanimities, or rubber-stamping the declarations of popes: the Church's foundation doctrines emerged—and emerge—by debate, conflict, and eventually consensus: painful and costly processes which may take decades and even centuries to crystallize. The nineteenth century Ultramontanes, like their twenty-first-century descendents, yearned for history without bewilderment or tears, and looked to the tradition, and the *magisterium* as the mouthpiece of tradition, for a living oracle which could short-circuit human confusion and limitation: it was and is the attempt to confront the uncertainties of our age with instant assurance, revelation on tap. But what such a project amounts to, in fact, is the effective abolition of tradition, abandoning attention to the complex and not always harmonious chorus of our shared past, and replacing it with the monotone voice of present authority.[92]

With so much in common between the Roman and Anglican traditions, I am puzzled by our divisions. I realize that this call for rapprochement and humble receiving of one another in love seems naive and is anathema to some people, who make one issue the litmus test of orthodoxy. I remember the relentless talk about the necessity of a nuclear freeze in the Diocese of New York in the 1970s. This, rather than belief in the resurrection, was the litmus test of orthodoxy among the liberals in those days. Now, it seems to be either gay rights or concern for climate change. (For the conservatives it's sex and a literal interpretation of Scripture.) The nuclear freeze, gay rights, and concern for the environment are all vitally important, but these concerns flow from who we think God is. Does it necessarily follow that if American and Canadian Anglicans are marginalized by the rest of the Anglican Communion we are necessarily being "prophetic"? It may be true, but not necessarily. Each group seems to have its own peculiar litmus test for orthodoxy.

Looking at the Big Picture

To be fair, I think it is the peculiar vocation of some to be uncompromising about the issues in front of us. The trouble is that with all this fragmentation and tribalism, there aren't enough of us who respond to the call to hold the *larger* vision in our minds and see that our form of spiritual obedience is to help maintain our fragile institutions against the "idiocy" of fragmentation.

What about the "big picture"? Ian McEwan in *Saturday* writes of the new "sincerely godless generation." The hero Henry, thinking about his ironically named son Theo for whom the question of God doesn't come up, says,

> No one in his bright, plate-glass, forward-looking school ever asked him to pray, or sing an impenetrable cheery hymn. There's no entity for him to doubt. Theo's aphorism is: "The bigger you think, the crappier it looks. When we go on about the big things, the political situation, global warming, world poverty, it all looks really terrible, with nothing getting better, nothing to look forward to. But when I think smaller, closer in—you know, a girl I've just met . . . or snowboarding next month, then it looks great. So this is going to be my motto—think small."[93]

It's hard to have a vision of the "big picture" even as we battle with the particular issues that confront us day to day. The art of conversation helps us do both.

Conversation is essential, but it should not be confused with superficial chat. The encounter can be passionate and confrontational or it can be affirming and nurturing. We know that mere exchange of information isn't enough to bring us together. But neither is communication. We need, instead, the kind of conversation that leads to affiliation and alignment so that words can be translated into actions for the common good.

I grew up in the Anglican tradition as received by the Church of England. The Church of England was all over the map theologically and liturgically, and it was possible to experience the whole ecumenical movement without leaving the Church of England. I started as an evangelical Protestant (the tradition I honor because it brought me to Christ) and ended up a reformed Catholic (the tradition I honor because it sustains my commitment). Underneath it all was the affirmation of the Christian character: extolling simple virtues of telling the truth, saying your prayers, reading the Bible, breaking bread, and—yes—being kind and decent. What is disturbing to me is that this generous and broad view of our faith is in jeopardy. It isn't easy for me—given the recent culture wars in both church and state—to recognize what I took for granted as authentic Anglicanism. Like "art"—I don't quite know what it is but I know it when I see it. I saw and heard Anglicanism in the evangelical preaching of John Stott, the vicar of All Souls, Langham Place, and in the Catholic vision of the Cowley and Mirfield Fathers. We seem to like anything (for example, labeling) that helps us bypass thought.

Reverent Agnosticism

The late Alan Richardson, the dean of York and my old teacher, told us that about many things—not *everything*—we should be reverent agnostics. We should stand before mystery and be willing "not to know." To me, this is a Christian spiritual virtue, which many of my fellow Christians find intolerable. Labeling is believed to be essential. Black-and-white clarity is mandatory. W. S. Gilbert wrote in the operetta *Iolanthe*:

> I often think it's comical
> How Nature always does contrive
> That every boy and every gal
> That's born into the world alive
> Is either a little Liber-al
> Or else a little Conserva-tive.

These lines are an amusing reminder that it's almost impossible to go through the world without being labeled. Years ago it got back to me that an evangelical rector in New York had said of me, "The trouble with Alan Jones is that he's a Platonist," by which he meant that I was influenced by Eastern

Orthodox theology, especially the Cappadocian Fathers. I was flattered. Scratch an Anglican and you will find a Platonist! I was also labeled once as "too Benedictine," by which was meant that I emphasized the balance in the spiritual life between private prayer, the Daily Office, and sharing in the Eucharist. Another compliment. But what of the criticism that I am really an agnostic?

Thomas Huxley coined the word in 1869.

> When I reached intellectual maturity, and began to ask myself whether I was an atheist, a theist, or a pantheist; a materialist or an idealist; a Christian or a freethinker, I found that the more I learned and reflected, the less ready was the answer; until at last I came to the conclusion that I had neither art nor part with any of these denominations, except the last. The one thing in which most of these good people were agreed was the one thing in which I differed from them. They were quite sure that they had attained a certain "gnosis"—had more or less successfully solved the problem of existence; while I was quite sure I had not, and had a pretty strong conviction that the problem was insoluble.[94]

Early in life, he says, he perceived that society regards an unlabeled person as a potential menace, in the way that the police regard an unmuzzled dog. Hence the term agnostic suggested itself to him as descriptive of this difference, and he accordingly adopted it as a label.

My friend Sam Keen and I are poles apart theologically and liturgically (he'd say he hasn't a liturgical bone in his body), but we agree on the importance of a certain kind of agnosticism.

> Far from being irreverent, cynical, or crypto-atheistic, agnosticism may be rooted in an unshakable sense of the sacred. My brand of agnosticism involves a constant dialogue with religious yearning and an ultimate concern with the questions that have animated the great exemplars of faith in the Buddhist, Taoist, Jewish, and Christian traditions. I dwell among these questions: How do we live in a time of the absence or silence of God? How do we retain a sense of the sacredness in our lives? How do we discover values and visions that transcend the myopia of ego, tribe, corporation, and nation? How and to whom do I sing praises when I am in exile? To whom do I address my prayers of thanksgiving and supplication? What does it mean to consider something sacred, or holy?[95]

It seems to me that Anglican orthodoxy has an element of agnosticism in it because it combines the reverence for mystery, the commitment to conversation, with the willingness to wait in the cloud of unknowing. This kind of reverent agnosticism seems to have as much to do with temperament as with conviction. This approach, I know, seems ridiculous not only to certain kinds of Roman Catholics and Protestants but also to a significant number of Anglicans. These Anglicans of both the right and left, to my mind, need to go back to their roots. Anglicans are agnostics about many things. They know the church can err and make mistakes.

Defying Definition

In a church that's open to the possibility of erring, we are also open in the way we understand doctrine. And that makes it difficult to define exactly what orthodox Anglicanism is. As we have seen, this broad view of Christian commitment is easily caricatured as flabby and vapid. The myth about Anglicans is that we're not big on dogma, we don't believe a great deal, and we're not required to believe anything in particular. We're the Zen Buddhists of the West (actually a label I like). What else would you expect, wrote a recent commentator (a convert to conservative Roman Catholicism who despises our tradition), from a church "founded on a king's lust!" Another convert to "the true unerring Church" described himself as "a former member of a self-satisfied liberal Protestant club." When Anglicans hear comments like these, it's hard to resist the temptation to strike back with cracks about the Borgia popes or the Avignon papacy. It is true in one sense that we aren't big on doctrine-as-propositions, but we are big on worship. Our beliefs are enshrined in our prayer books. We are a liturgical and nonconfessional church. A good illustration of the absence of definition in doctrine is that of the atonement. Although some of us are wedded to a particular theory, it has been "the wisdom of the Church to leave the matter of the saving efficacy of the Cross as an undefined mystery and thus open to a range of theological reflections."[96] While some think of the cross as punishment, others think of it as the obedient self-offering of love.

Like Archbishop Peter Carnley, I don't see myself as either a theological liberal or as an advocate of a tradition that can never err. Still less are we Anglicans biblical fundamentalists. We see ourselves as "progressive orthodox" or "progressive traditionalists." In much the same way, Sam Lloyd, dean of the National Cathedral, at his installation in Washington, called for a generous vision of our faith. We offer a different voice from that of liberals and conservatives.

As Peter Carnley points out, "The fear of liberalism in the Church, understood as a bland presentation of the Gospel without a clear cutting edge, appears to bulk large amongst contemporary conservative-minded Anglicans as a fundamental enemy which they must confront."[97]

But liberal or conservative aren't the only two choices we can make. Somewhere between "liberalism" and "literalism" there are a number of other positions. Each of the poles is extreme and unacceptable. The "tolerant and liberal West," on the one hand, with its trashy culture and the kind of tolerance that cannot sustain the world community or eliminate terrorism. (Indeed, our excessive tolerance—even permissiveness—in Western culture surely triggers revulsion and hatred in other parts of the world, and the cultural trash we export invites it.) Liberal religion tends to be a privatized spirituality based on mutual treaties of noninterference. Indeed, the phony dualism between religion and spirituality seems to be at the heart of the "liberal" point of view, which tolerates religion as long as it's a kind of hobby. On the other hand, conservative religion tends toward closed communities with excommunicating power.

Both the conservative and the liberal camps offer a mixed bag of pluses and minuses. Though I may not appreciate the theology of the conservatives, I like the fact that they refuse to allow religion to be marginalized or trivialized. I believe they're right to resist the privatization of religion. While conservatives insist that morality is not a purely private matter, "liberal" morality tends to be simply a matter of personal decision rather than a matter of rational argument in the public realm. But from the Christian point of view, there is no such thing as a totally "private" act. The positive side of liberalism is that it advocates an ethic of aspiration rather than prescription.

Liberals also criticize our mythic individualism. Robert Bellah's *Habits of the Heart* (1985) is, in part, an indictment of an individualism gone rancid. We mustn't give up the public conversation and our commitment to the commonwealth. Those of us on the many sides of issues need to renew our determination to be in conversation about shared morality and shared values. Identity politics (in religion and in politics) of mere assertion reinforce fragmentation. It simply isn't true that one view is as good as another, and that, therefore, everything is to be tolerated; after all, who's to say your values are better than mine?

Carnley is clear on this point. "The idea of moral truths," he writes, "tends to go out the window in liberal democratic society. We are schooled instead simply in liberal-minded tolerance, the tolerance of a plethora of alternative view points, as though one is as good as another."[98] We don't think flogging, for example, is a good idea. It's not that there should be a law against it (although, perhaps, there should) but that we have no means of intelligent conversation about such things without one side screaming, "Intolerance! You have no right to tell me how to live my life." No, but our Christian faith, meant to be lived out in community, teaches us that our actions are not merely private matters. Each of our actions concerns us all. Society has a legitimate interest in not "tolerating" the tawdry, the grotesque, the antihuman. And if there's no consensus about what is tawdry, grotesque, and antihuman, then let's be committed to a heated but civil conversation about it.

The need becomes more intense the more multicultural we become. Cross-cultural conversation is essential. We need a genuine meeting of cultures, where differences aren't merely tolerated but celebrated—a conversation in which we are open to change our minds and modify our views. The tragedy here is that many of us seem to have given up the search for a public truth. Conservatives may try, though they tend not to respect or listen to other voices and there seems to be no vigorous countervailing voice from the liberal side. As Carnley points out, "Strident assertion and marching with placards tend to replace reasoned community conversation and debate." I still trust there's a critical mass of "people of good will" who have identified the soul-sickness of our culture—the diseases of Western liberal democracies:

> Youth suicide, the widespread prevalence of depression, the ubiquitous use of antidepressants, endemic child abuse, inequitable distribution of wellbeing between rich and poor, drug and alcohol abuse, and its associated crime and violence [the degradation of the environment], and the ensuing need for security systems just about everywhere these days to protect us, not from international terrorism, but from ourselves.[99]

Seeking Peace

We are at war with one another. One of the challenges of Anglican orthodoxy is not only to establish a truce but to seek real peace among the many contentious factions. We can do this in a number of ways.

First, our task may well be to act as a sign of contradiction by questioning the underpinning of Western liberal democratic society as a fundamentally incoherent path to self-destruction that has transformed us from neighbors into consumers. In this atmosphere, individual rights always trump the greater good to the detriment of all. But we forget that not all freedoms are of equal value and individual rights and freedoms aren't absolute. They have to be balanced by community interests. For orthodox Christians, the doctrine of the holy and undivided Trinity is a gift that helps us conceive what a truly free and open society might look like—in radical contrast to the doctrine of the autonomous individual beloved by the liberal democracies.

Next, we must realize that to be a person is to be in communion. In A.D. 374, Basil the Great in his treatise *On the Holy Spirit*,[100] spoke not so much of three persons in one substance as three persons in one communion. "The Trinity points to a social ideal and political agenda at variance with most of our social and political arrangements. So while individual rights are important to us, we cannot stop there. We have to talk about responsibilities towards others. The vision is mutual interdependence by self-gift." That's why the church is called to be fully ecumenical and charged to listen respectfully to what God is trying to tell us through other faith traditions.

Next we need to renew our commitment in the Anglican communion to internal ecumenism. We would do well to pledge to each other that we would not be schismatics. Some will accuse others of sacrificing truth for unity, but I believe a greater truth is served when our primary commitment to Christ keeps us at the table. We need ways to demonstrate our love for one another and for Jesus.

Anglican Progressive Orthodoxy

All of this, we hope, will lead to what is being called Anglican progressive orthodoxy. What does that look like? We've already cited the first three characteristics—a reverence for the mystery of God and a suspicion of truth in the form of verbal propositions, a commitment to listen and be in conversation, and a willingness not to have to know everything.

Our orthodoxy cannot do without language but language alone is inadequate, so when we speak of God we should speak humbly and haltingly, for the God who is *revealed* in Christ is still a mystery. But, let's be clear: Anglican orthodox theology is not without content. It insists that this transcendent God is *real*. God is not simply an idea—not even a good one. Belief isn't something made up from our heads. Because words are inadequate doesn't mean that there is no objective reality or that we have nothing to say.

Instead, Anglican orthodoxy holds two truths before us in tension and insists that these truths are held together. It is not a matter of either-or but of both-and. Gregory Palamas, the fourteenth-century monk and theologian, wrote that "the most venerable theologians—Athanasius, Basil, Gregory of Nyssa, John Chrysostom, Maximus—teach us two things. First they tell us that the divine essence is incommunicable; then, that it is in some way communicable: they tell us that we participate in the nature of God, and that we do not participate in it at all. We must, therefore, hold both assertions, and set them together as the rule of the true faith."[101] Two truths are the very backbone of our orthodoxy: one, God is inexhaustible and unknowable; and two, this inexhaustible and unknowable God has been revealed to us in Jesus Christ. According to Gregory, even though we cannot "know" God, we can experience the divine through sacraments and mystical prayer.

The late Henri de Lubac, S.J., wrote of the same fundamental paradox when it comes to our self-understanding. Human nature has an unstable

> "ontological constitution" which makes it at once something greater and something less than itself. Hence that kind of dislocation, that mysterious lameness, due not merely to sin, but primarily and more fundamentally to be a creature made out of nothing which, astound-

ingly, touches God . . . At once, and inextricably both "nothing" and "image"; fundamentally nothing, yet nonetheless substantially image.[102]

For de Lubac, Catholicism is social at the very heart of its mystery and dogma. But it is Trinitarian. There is an equal emphasis on solitude and solidarity, mysticism and community. There are solitary and social dimensions to being human. The source of both is God. The crucial place of solitude is in the emergence of selfhood.

The trouble is that in times of stress and controversy we cannot bear the paradox at the heart of our faith. We become impatient with the mystery at its heart. We are intolerant of contradiction. Henri de Lubac's classic text *The Mystery of the Supernatural* is one for our times. He calls us to struggle to hold the contradictions—authority and freedom, Bible and church, the Word eternal yet begotten, a finality that has no end—together. "A synthesis indeed; but for our natural intellect, it is a synthesis of paradox before being one of enlightenment."[103]

We are at each other's throats when we should be on our knees before the Christian mystery. We see something of the theological intelligence and spiritual depth of a de Lubac in the Anglican tradition in, for example, someone like John Donne, who understood our unstable ontological constitution, the dislocation, the mysterious lameness, what it was to be at once both *nothing* and *image*. It is impossible for those of us for whom paradox is a fire that burns within us to slip into an easy conceptualizing of reality, to transmute faith into a few propositions. The temptation is to come to an easy solution by coming down on one side of the mystery or the other: A human being is *either* nothing *or* image; we can't be both. Orthodoxy demands we hold both in tension. That's why orthodoxy, properly understood, is an open and dynamic way of believing—a spiritual adventure.

John Donne's Anglicanism exhibited a compassionate detachment to "see all things despoyl'd of fallacies." This involved hard intellectual discipline. Since intellect and emotion, in Donne, were so contracted that one infused and informed the other, the discipline of the intellect involved the stripping of the self. Stripping the intellect of pedantry and mere cleverness could be done only by a spirit that was recollected in meditation, in prayer, in spiritual discipline. Without that stripping down, the theologian becomes a "spungie slacke Divine," an intellectual and spiritual parasite, a plagiarist of the soul, living vicariously off the hard-won scholarship and the soul's anguish of others.[104]

Anglican orthodoxy, therefore, begins and ends in prayer, in silence before the mystery. It is not anti-intellectual but insists on the joining of intellect with emotion, of praying, as the Eastern tradition has it, with the mind in the heart.

True orthodoxy requires freedom. Belief cannot be coerced. My first test of anyone's orthodoxy is a question: "If you were in charge, would I be safe? Would there be room for me?" If the answer is yes, we can argue with love in our eyes. John Henry Newman wrote, "it was absurd to argue men, as to torture them, into believing." Newman is an important figure for us because he champions for both Anglicans and Roman Catholics a view of doctrine that is always mysterious because our information is incomplete. Doctrine is the first word, not the last word, about the mystery. It is a platform from which we can leap into it. For Newman, mystery was the badge and emblem of orthodoxy. "No revelation can be complete and systematic . . . Religious Truth is neither light nor darkness, but both together."[105] *Revelation is the disclosure of mystery.* This is the key. Again, this isn't reveling in ambiguity but rather has practical implications. We cannot, from this, build a theological system as an instrument of power with which to bully and bludgeon others.

We are, if you will, Erasmian Catholics. In a letter to Cardinal Campegio early in 1529, Erasmus wrote:

> Every definition is a misfortune. . . . True religion is peace, and we cannot have peace unless we leave the conscience unshackled on obscure points. . . . If we want the truth, every man ought to be free to say what he thinks without fear. If the advocates of one side are to be rewarded with mitres and the advocates of the other with rope or stakes truth will not be heard.[106]

Having said that, I am conservative in that I am committed to the fundamental tenets of the catholic and apostolic faith of the undivided Christian Church. I'm not free to make it up as I go along. As Peter Carnley insists, "[Orthodoxy] has nothing to do with the liberalism of the post-Enlightenment Western world which would leave all matters of belief and value to be decided by the autonomous individual. [We are] suspicious of the overconfident use of reason that characterizes liberalism in its quest to accommodate faith to the wisdom of the world."[107] St. Gregory of Nyssa, like Gregory Palamas, reminds us that "we know that He is, but deny not that we are ignorant of the definition of His essence."[108]

With this as the foundation of our orthodoxy, we shouldn't be surprised that Anglicans don't take to infallibility very well—whether it be that of the pope or the Bible. The Bible is very much a polarizing agent in this current climate. There are Bible-believing Christians and the rest of us. This doesn't get us very far, because it begs the question of interpretation. Archbishop Carnley puts it bluntly:

To claim that only those who promiscuously skate over differences and discrepancies in the texts can really be regarded as 'Bible-believing' is offensive to those who believe that the true message of the Bible can only be discerned, not by following the letter, but with the help of the Spirit, as the Word of God is discerned in and through the diversity of faith perspectives found within the canon of scripture.[109]

The sad state of affairs now is that those who think that they are the only ones who take the Bible seriously as the literal Word of God dump the rest of us in the "liberal" camp.

We must never forget that for Anglicans, theology always gives way to the impulse to worship. We move into prayer and into silence. It's no wonder that we've spent more time producing prayer books than defining doctrines. Mystery, silence, conversation, freedom leads us to worship. Theology can be done only on our knees.

There is yet another characteristic of Anglican orthodoxy. We believe that we don't stand before the world as if we have nothing to learn. We do not have the answer to every conceivable question. We feel no pressure to keep on correcting others. As Peter Carnley eloquently puts it:

We can live comfortably with diversity because we acknowledge that all attempts to express the divine will in some way fall short of absolute truth. We do not approach the practice of religion, therefore, as though it involved having all the answers, because we do not see life primarily as a problem to be solved. Rather we see ourselves as being on an open-ended journey into a future to which we are called by God, a journey of faith and hope, in which there is always something new to learn, a mind-set to be expanded, a perception of things to be stretched, a deeper wisdom to be discerned.[110]

This is progressive and dynamic orthodoxy.

PART IV

Anglicanism's Future? The Clue Is in Our Past

PART IV

Anglicanism's Future? The Clue Is in Our Past

And all the wickedness in the world that man might work or think is no more to the mercy of God than a live coal dropped into the sea.
—William Langland, c. A.D. 1400.

What is that ultimate and unutterable mystery which engulfs our being, and whence we take our rise, and wither our journey leads us?
—Vatican II: Declaration on the Relationship of the Church to Non-Christian Religions

I wonder sometimes if being an Anglican is a matter of temperament. Anglicanism is very English. Charles Williams, lecturing in Paris in 1938, claimed that the French have a tendency to say Yes *or* No and the English to say Yes *and* No! He told them, "I think it would perhaps be useful if we did not blame each other." The English mind, with its passion for compromise, seeks a union of opposites, even when they seem irreconcilable. This is, evidently, infuriating to the French mind. Charles Williams claimed this about the English: "We perish for things in which we believe and yet not believe," willingly offering ourselves as martyrs for things about which we are skeptical. He says the two traditions of "Yes-and-No" and Yes-or-No" need to forgive each other. The real difficulty is to endure our being tolerated *by* other people. Because I abhor conflict and always look for reconciliation, I have sometimes been accused of being double-minded. I take the accusation seriously. It should be clear by now that, for me, heresy is a far less serious sin than schism. This is very English and Anglican. Historian Jacques Barzun writes this about Walter Bagehot, the nineteenth-century English journalist:

> His singular genius derives from his double vision. In any conflict of persons or ideas he was always able to see that neither side was per-

verse or stupid, but had reasons for militancy; and he entered not only into these reasons but also into the feelings attached. This is a rare talent, especially when it does not lead to shilly-shallying in the double-viewers own course of action.[111]

I don't claim to be there but I aspire to Bagehot's gift of being able to enter sympathetically into opposing views without compromising my own position. Bagehot's great comment was, "Unfortunately mysticism is true." It is too bad, he meant, for the person always after the main chance. "Realism" is not enough. We are held within a mystery that we can neither comprehend nor manipulate.

Learning from the Past

I believe Anglicanism has an important role to play in this present century. In fact, it may only just be coming into its own. In the upheavals of the sixteenth and seventeenth centuries in England, people exhibited a remarkable combination of qualities (the ability to bear paradox and contradiction for the sake of the larger mystery) for the building of community, and those are the very qualities we need today. A. M. Allchin, referring to George Herbert, writes, "It was in such a school of thought, which sought to escape from the increasing rigidity of current controversies by an appeal to the method and spirit of the early Christian centuries, that George Herbert was formed."[112] Here are some of the characteristics:

1. The willingness to question, joined to a deep power of affirmation.
2. The appreciation of the uniqueness of the individual together with an appreciation of the value of what is corporate and traditional.
3. The intuitive understanding that the Christian life is not either inward or outward; it is inescapably both.
4. The ability to speak "with the old authority and the new culture" (T. S. Eliot).
5. The eagerness to be spiritually honest in not being willing to disguise the element of conflict in our relationship with God. A. M. Allchin writes of George Herbert, "He does not hide his moments of rebellion, the temptations to doubt, the periods of dryness and deadness."
6. The openness of a discerning heart—one that knows what matters and what doesn't. "Without evading the complexity of things, without glossing over the fragility and brokenness of human experience in time, he [George Herbert] managed to reaffirm the great unities of Christian life and prayer."[113]
7. The remarkable capacity to hold together things often believed to be separable or opposed to one another.

The historian and exponent of both Celtic and Benedictine spiritualities so central for Anglicans, Esther de Waal, affirms that we are called to be a people of the imagination, "a people for whom prayer is elemental, corporate, heroic, imaginative; for whom life is an adventure; above all a people who are at home in and with themselves."[114] She wants companions who do not try to escape from themselves or from God. In order to enter into this new kind of community we must rediscover the visual and the nonverbal; we must be willing to be confronted by the power of image and symbol— the water of baptism; the bread and wine of the banquet to which everyone is invited.

It's time to make a new beginning by taking a fresh look at the past. Esther de Waal writes beautifully of encountering (without idealizing) in the Celtic tradition of Christianity "something basic, primal, fundamental, universal. I am taken back beyond the party labels and the denominational divisions of the Church today, beyond the divides of the Reformation, or the schism of East and West. I am also taken beyond the split of intellect and feeling, of mind and heart. . . ."[115] This look at our past can take us into a new realm of wholeness that encompasses all tribes, all tongues, all peoples. All of us are really on one journey, both shared and personal. Are we a community, de Waal challenges us to ask, ready to go wherever the Spirit might take us?

She highlights two phrases in the tradition: "[W]e are . . . 'guests of the world,' seeking places of resurrection, the resurrected self, the true self in Christ, which is for all of us our true home. And we do it all . . . for the love of Christ." The Celtic view of pilgrimage seems to us purposeless, drifting without oars over the sea—with the Spirit of God as the wind. But the seekers embarked on their pilgrimage for the love of God, caring not where they drifted because they knew they were guests of the world, traveling only for the love of Christ.

Voices from Our Tradition

We need to know about these roots of our tradition. The study of history is essential. The trouble is, many liberals don't care about it and many conservatives don't really know it. Both sides seem to have short memories. Listen to the following voices from our tradition—breathtakingly sane and generous. Their words give us some idea of that elusive thing—the Anglican ethos—and give us direction for the future.

First, consider the words of John Jewel (1522–1571) in his *Apology of the Church of England* (1562) on the Eucharist.

> We say that the bread and wine are the holy and heavenly mysteries of the body of Christ, and that in them Christ himself, the true bread of

eternal life, is so exhibited to us as present, that we do by faith truly take his body and blood; and yet at the same time we speak not this so as if we thought the nature of the bread and wine were totally changed and abolished, as many in the last age have dreamt, and as yet could never agree among themselves about this dream. For neither did Christ ever design that the wheaten bread should change its nature, and assume a new kind of divinity, but rather that it might change us.[116]

I invite you, also, to contemplate Richard Hooker's maxim in his *Of the Laws of Ecclesiastical Polity* (1593 and following): "So natural is the union of religion with justice, that we may boldly assert that there is neither where there is not both." Think about that.

Think, too, about the crucible of history that forged our tradition. The mid-seventeenth century was hardly a bland and flabby time. Imagine what it was like in the 1640s to see some of the Puritans go around smashing statues and destroying great works of Christian art. A 1643 report by one Puritan group noted: "We brake down twelve superstitious pictures, and took two popish inscriptions, four cherubims, and a holy water font from the porch door.... At Little Mary's ... We brake down sixty superstitious pictures, some popes and crucifixes, and God the Father sitting in a chair holding a glass." St. Paul's Cathedral was used as a cavalry stable, another cathedral's font became a watering trough. Joseph Hall (1574–1656), bishop of Norwich, wrote this, after that great cathedral was trashed by Puritans.

Lord, what work was here, what clattering of glass, what beating down of walls, what tearing of monuments, what pulling down of seats, what wresting out of irons and brass from windows and graves, what defacing of arms, ... and what hideous triumph on the market day before all the country, when, in a kind of sacrilegious and profane procession, all the organ pipes, vestments, both copes and surplices, together with the leaden Cross which had been newly sawn down from over the green yard pulpit, and the service books and singing books that could be had, were carried to the fire in the marketplace.... Neither was it any news ... to have the Cathedral now open on all sides, to be filled with musketeers ... drinking and tobaccoing as freely as if it had turned ale-house.

We would do well to remember our past. In the 1640s and 1650s there was toleration for all but Roman Catholics and Anglicans. Episcopacy was abolished in 1644, along with all forms of church structure, including cathedral chapters and deans. The Book of Common Prayer was made illegal.

Almost a third of the clergy were thrown out of their parishes. The observance of Christmas Day was forbidden.

On Christmas Day 1658, John Evelyn (1620–1706) and his wife were caught attending a Prayer Book service at Exeter Chapel in the Strand. Evelyn wrote in his diary:

> Sermon ended, as the celebrant was giving up the Holy Sacrament, the chapel was surrounded by soldiers, and all the communicants and assembly surprised and kept prisoners by them, some in the house, others carried away. . . . When I came before them they took my name and abode, examined me why contrary to an ordinance made than none should any longer observe the superstitious time of the Nativity (so esteemed by them), I did offend, and particularly be at Common Prayers, which they told me was but the mass in English. . . . As we went up to receive the Sacrament the miscreants held their muskets against us as if they would have shot us at the altar. . . .

Later, alas, the Anglicans took their revenge in the harsh laws of the Restoration. Some Anglicans were distressed by the bigotry and idiocy of their own church. William Warburton, bishop of Gloucester from 1760 to 1779, wrote: "The Church, like the Ark of Noah, is worth saving; not for the sake of the unclean beasts and vermin that almost filled it, and probably made most noise and clamor in it; but for the little corner of rationality that was as much distressed by the stink within as by the tempest without." Rationality in this context sounds attractive.

Nearer our own time, Anglicans were privileged to have some great archbishops of Canterbury. Here's William Temple (Archbishop of Canterbury, 1942–44) writing as early as 1908:

> The whole desire of the Church has been to offer the fullness of God's help to every soul but never to dictate to any soul precisely how that soul may best receive the benefit. It sets a high standard for the individual member. No doubt it involves comparative failure, for very many who might, by a more strict and military discipline, have been led to a fuller use of all the means of grace than in fact they practice under the Anglican system.

And the voices of two more recent archbishops of Canterbury encourage us. First, Robert Runcie:

> We must never make the survival of the Anglican Communion an end in itself, the Churches of the Anglican Communion have never

claimed to be more than a part of the one holy catholic and apostolic Church. Anglicanism, as a separate denomination, has a radically provisional character which must never be allowed to be obscured.

And Michael Ramsey:

> For while the Anglican Church is vindicated by its place in history, with a strikingly balanced witness to Gospel and Church and sound learning, its greater vindication lies in its pointing through its own history to something of which it is a fragment. Its credentials are its incompleteness, with the tension and travail in its soul. It is clumsy and untidy, it baffles neatness and logic. For it is sent not to commend itself as "the best type of Christianity," but by its very brokenness to point to the universal church wherein all have died.[117]

The Voice of John Donne

Finally, here's my own love letter to Anglicanism, inspired by John Donne. Some years ago I wrote an article as part of a volume of essays in honor of the late Canon Edward Nason West of the Cathedral of St. John the Divine in New York City. I chose to write about John Donne, the metaphysical poet and dean of St. Paul's in the first part of the seventeenth century.

John Donne is fascinating for us because his own person was the battleground of the forces of change struggling for control in his age. He assisted at the birth of what we call the modern world. Like us, he lived in a world that was dying. Like us, he sensed the birth tremors of a new thing. He lived during the birth of modern astronomy, which not only exploded the medieval cosmology but caused a profound upheaval in the human psyche, in human self-understanding. The great literature of his time helped people to adjust to their changing world—Shakespeare and Milton described the coming realities using the terminology of the old cosmology; and Donne himself, in his own writing, took up the theological and personal issues surfacing as a result of Baconian science. Was not Christianity too provincial, too mundane, he asked, to cope with the emerging "brave new world"? Were not humanity's moral resources too weak to cope with seventeenth-century "future shock"?

To read John Donne, particularly the sermons, in the light of the present stresses in the Anglican Communion and the Episcopal Church, is an exhilarating experience. Donne was a man afflicted with that peculiarly human disease, transcendence. For him, human beings are oriented toward mystery. He was convinced that human beings carry around within them, at their deepest, a terrible yet marvelous "otherness," and that this otherness was forever calling them "to be," recreating them "out of nothing." Donne, then, was driven by the conviction that there is always more, that we are called continually to go beyond ourselves.

Donne had, in true Augustinian fashion, looked sin and death in the face; he had lusted and loved; he had seen the vanity of this world and caught a glimpse of its promised transfiguration. Like Augustine, he was a doctor of grace, living on borrowed time, a Lazarus who had come back from the dead. Mortality was real, desperately real, but resurrection was a present event. No wonder his sermons burst with energy, with impatience, and with compassion. He was a living icon to his age of transcendence, a sign that there was more, not only above and beyond us but also within us, in the dark richness of what a later poet was to call the "inscape."[118]

Donne was not only a Christian; he was an Anglican. This is an important particular, since he lived out Christianity in its Anglican form. The spirit of Anglicanism is best discovered in the lives of its most distinguished practitioners, but while there are those who equal John Donne, there are none who surpass him. He expresses Anglicanism at its best, not the woolly compromise of the *via media*, but the comprehensiveness, the compassion, and the liberality of the *via regia* (the royal way). In his life and in his writings, he lived out the theology of Anglicanism—incarnational, pragmatic, functional, earthy, but always aware that this world has a transcendent reference.

Anglicanism as lived by John Donne was not the safe, stodgy thing that some have mistaken for the true marks of English Christianity. To be a vigorous Anglican in the seventeenth century was an exciting and unnerving enterprise. Anglicans then, as now, resisted ready-made answers. These ready-made answers were to be found uncompromisingly in Geneva and Rome, in churches that would not and could not err. Anglicans were determined to find another way. The Caroline Divines (those who lived in the tumultuous time of Charles I—people like John Donne, George Herbert, Jeremy Taylor, and Lancelot Andrewes) look solid and attractive behind the haze of seventeenth-century prose, but we easily forget that an archbishop could lose his head, and a king his, for Anglican principles. Donne lived through the decades from the Civil War, the execution of a king and an archbishop, to the persecution of the church; he lived amid the extremism that was Anglicanism's cradle. The choices were Geneva or Rome or the rationalism of the new science. Anglicans, then and now, reject all three.

Baconian rationalism held no attractions for Donne, not because he refused to accept the new science, but because he quickly realized that descriptions of phenomena actually explain nothing. Explanations merely describe phenomena in a new way, however useful and illuminating it may be. In its limited fashion, the new mode of looking at the world was perfectly acceptable to Donne, but he resisted the reductionist tendencies of the new science that excluded mystery, lost the transcendental dimension, and missed the interconnectedness of things, leaving everything dead and spiritless, robbed of significance. Donne's age, like our own, cried out for a "metaphysic," an overview of the world to harmonize all the discordant elements and make sense of all the disordered fragments of experience. "Metaphysical" had a special meaning in the century. Historian Basil Willey explains that "metaphysical" meant

> the capacity to live in divided and distinguished worlds, and to pass freely to and from between one and the other, to be capable of many and varied responses to experience, instead of being confined to a few stereotyped ones. . . . The point about these different worlds was not that they were divided, but that they were simultaneously available . . . I think that something of the peculiar quality of the "metaphysical" mind is due to the fact of its not being finally committed to any one world. Instead, it could hold them all in a loose synthesis together, yielding itself, as only a mind in free poise can, to the passion of detecting analogies and correspondences between them.[119]

In our chaotic pluralism, we need a new breed of metaphysicians who will be possessed by the passion for analogies and correspondences; men and women with the ability to move freely between and live simultaneously in different worlds. Donne could do this. He refused to capitulate to the either/or mentality that Gregory of Palamas so roundly criticized. He was resolved to be a modern—but a *believing* modern. His was a metaphysic not built up out of speculative philosophy that sought to disguise the untidy paradoxes of existence, but one formed out of having experienced these "contrareities" in his personal history. He struggled toward a unified vision but came to see that contrariness and ambiguity are in the very fiber of things. The elemental fact of ambivalence, he discovered, is that it demands coexistence and complementarity.

The sense of complementarity, the apprehension of the interconnectedness of things, comes at a high price. Donne's intuition; his "psychic sense of smell"; and his second religion, friendship, transformed his cynicism into a healthy skepticism. In the end, he realized that the ambiguities of existence could only be resolved in the painful unitive experience of love. He was excited by his sense of the pervasive unity underlying phenomena. Donne reflects on his own experience, and that reflected experience becomes an icon through which he perceives all that there is: "I was built up scarce fifty years ago in my mother's womb, and I was cast down almost 6,000 years ago in Adam's loins. I was born in the last Age of the world and died in the first."[120]

His own experience serves as a beam of light to illuminate human history and ultimate reality. Donne was never embarrassed by the particular or

by the basic stuff of things. Earthiness does not cause the sacred to evapo-
rate. It is its prerequisite. Without clods of earth, without the flesh, spirit can
never have expression. Knowledge is "a terrestriall Spirit." Donne, the
learned doctor in divinitie, knew that no less than did Donne the lover: the
particularity of venereal pleasures in the early years served to reinforce the
use of the particular in his sermons, as dean of St. Paul's Cathedral in
London.

So there was in Donne an unusually creative unity of intellect and emotion. This is the heart of Donne's genius: his ability to translate thought into
feeling without degenerating into sentimentality. He did this by a painful
process of sifting and discrimination. Hence his thoughts were tested,
honed, assayed before they were transmuted into feeling. He was unafraid
intellectually.

> I throw my selfe down in my Chamber, and I call in, and invite God,
> and his Angels thither, and when they are there, I neglect God and his
> Angels, for the noise of a Flie, for the ratling of a Coach, for the whin-
> ing of a doore; I talke on, in the same posture of praying; Eyes lifted
> up; knees bowed downe; as though I prayed to God; and if God, or his
> Angels should aske me, when I thought last of God in that prayer, I
> cannot tell; sometimes I finde that I had forgot what I was about, but
> when I began to forget it I cannot tell. A memory of yesterdays pleas-
> ures, a feare of tomorrows dangers, a straw under my knee, a noise in
> mine eare, a light in mine eye, an anything, a nothing, a fancy, a
> Chimera in my braine, troubles me in my prayer. So certainely is there
> nothing, nothing in spirituall things, perfect in this world.[121]

What Donne says about prayer can be said about dogma. There is "nothing in spirituall things, perfect in this world." There are no perfect creeds, for-
mularies, articles, or confessions. Meaning trapped in language can easily slip
away. This does not mean that nothing meaningful can be said, nothing significant affirmed. This doesn't mean that God is not to be trusted. It simply
means that reality will not be trapped.

Donne's belief in God was certain, but it was a certainty springing from
sensibility, from Donne's having "a direct sensuous apprehension of thought."
He *felt* his thoughts. He did his thinking as he did his praying, with his mind
in his heart. He could be as hard on the intellectuals tending toward atheism
as he was on the Puritans and Papists veering always toward dogmatism.
"Poore intricated soule! Riddling, perplexed, labyrinthicall soule. Thou
couldest not say, that thou beleevest not in God, if there were no God; If there
were no God, thou couldest not speake, thou couldest not thinke, not a word,
not a thought, no not against God."[122]

God was the prerequisite, then, even for doubting God's existence. Donne, the Augustinian, would always insist on the priority of God and the doctrine of prevenient grace—the grace of God that is before everything else—the prerequisite for our existence. But his hard-won new mode of sensibility would not allow dogma to degenerate into mere explanations of mysteries. This was his main quarrel with the church of his birth. Seventeenth-century Catholicism wanted to *explain* everything. Donne called it *quomodo* ("this is how it is") theology. He loathed *quomodo* theology that eviscerated mystery by a too-neat explanation and flattened out all untidy paradoxes. "He that can finde no comfort in this Doctrine . . . till he can expresse Quo Modo, robs himself of a great deale of peaceful refreshing."

Dominic Baker Smith writes:

It was the question of *quomodo* which elicited the fatal answer of transubstantiation, and to Donne the Roman Church, as he understood it, came to be the Church of *quomodo*, translating the Gospel into definitions and formulae that seemed indifferent to human response. In the same spirit he objects to an insensitive theology with sacraments *ex opere operato* [from the work performed] as automatic and self-contained means of grace.

Rome was too mechanistic, too regimented for Donne. The intimacy of the divine-human encounter was lost, forfeited in the intricacies of explanation, by seeking to "imprison Christ in *opere operato*." The Roman Catholic teaching that the grace of a sacrament is always conferred by the sacrament itself came to be interpreted in a mechanical, if not to say magical, way. *Ex opere operato* literally means "from the work performed."

Theology, *as explanation*, stultified the mind. "Rome has spoken, the matter is settled" doesn't sit well with Anglicans. So Donne preached: "To come to a doubt, and to a debatement in any religious duty, is the voyce of God in our conscience: Would you know the truth? Doubt, and then you will inquire."[123]

For Donne, we live within the mystery of God, which cannot be objectified. But within that mystery we can question, probe, examine, and come face-to-face with the mystery that is ourselves. In Dominic Baker-Smith's suggestive phrase, "The individual must expose himself to reality and this means ultimately to God with an arduous passivity." An arduous passivity: there is a phrase Donne could have understood and embraced. In a later age, Donne would have been called a Barthian, in this respect at least—before God we are nothing; that a person is created to be someone is a sheer act of unmerited grace. Life comes to us as gift not as right.

"At the centre of the self," writes Dominic Baker-Smith, "is memory, 'the Holy Ghost's Pulpit' containing the collective history that is the Bible and the private history that is the individual." Without recollection, both collective and personal, the soul has no room to grow. The model the Church of Rome offered did not do justice to the reality of a living organism in which the principles both of continuity and change were at work. Yet, Rome was powerful and articulate. It needed answering.

The locus classicus of Donne's Anglicanism is in his sermon preached on the Conversion of St. Paul, 1630. His text was Acts 23:6–7:

> But when Paul perceived that one part were Sadducees, and the other Pharisees, he cried out in the Council, Men and Brethren, I am a Pharisee, and the son of a Pharisee; of the hope and resurrection of the dead I am called in question. And when he had said so, there arose a dissention between the Pharisees and the Sadducees and the multitude was divided.

Donne was as politically astute as Paul and might have cried out, "I am a Catholic and the son of a Catholic! I am a Protestant too!" What united many of the Roman and Genevan persuasions was their common amazement and puzzlement at the Anglican position: the much-maligned *via media*. Here is Donne's brilliant exposition:

> Beloved, there are some things in which all Religions agree: The worship of God; The holiness of life; And therefore, if when I study this holinesse of life, and fast and pray, and submit my selfe to discreet, and medicinall mortifications, for the subduing of my body, any man will say, this is Papisticall, Papists doe this, it is a blessed Protestation, and no man is the lesse a Protestant, nor the worse a Protestant for making it. Men and brethren, I am a Papist, that is, I will fast and pray as much as any Papist, and enable myselfe for the service of my God, as seriously, as laboriously as any Papist. So, if when I startle and am affected at a blasphemous oath, as at a wound upon my Saviour, if when I avoyd the conversation of those men, that prophane the Lords day, any other will say to me, This is Puritanicall, Puritans do this, It is a blessed Protestation, and no man is the lesse a Protestant, nor the worse a Protestant for making it, Men and Brethren, I am a Puritan, that is, I wil endeavour to be pure, as my Father in heaven is pure, as far as any Puritan.[124]

This is a superb example of that elusive thing, Anglican style. It hinges on being able to tolerate a *may* where the dogmatist would demand a *must*: "Their may, came to a must, those things which were done before de facto, came at last to the articles of Faith, and de jure, must be beleeved and practised upon salvation. They chide us for going away, and they drove us away."[125]

It would help to focus Donne's "cosmic" Anglicanism by examining his doctrine of the church, whose sole object is to contemplate Christ clearly and uniformly. The dissension; the internecine war; the polemics of Rome, Geneva, and Canterbury—all these distressed him because they marred the face of Christ in the world. He knew too much of the theological warfare within the Roman Church to be persuaded that the sure ark of salvation was the bark of Peter. Rome could not come through with what she promised. Her claims regarding this life properly belonged to the life to come.

Donne believed that the task of the church was to make Christ visible to the world. If Rome wanted to impress Anglicans with her extravagant claims, she should first set her own house in order.

> Let me see a Dominican and a Jesuit reconciled, in doctrinall papistry, for free will and predestination. Let me see a French papist and an Italian papist reconciled in state papistry, for the Pope's jurisdiction. Let me see the Jesuits and the secular priests reconciled in England, and when they are reconciled to one another, let them presse reconciliation to their Church.[126]

We must remember that Donne was writing in the early seventeenth century: the century of Catholic killing Protestant, of Protestant killing Catholic, of Anglican killing Puritan, and of Puritan killing Anglican. It was tragic that Donne's countrymen were unable to receive his word. Perhaps we can hear it now over three and a half centuries later. It surely has an uncanny contemporary ring and speaks to the present need of the church to proclaim the uniqueness of Christ without lapsing into ecclesiastical megalomania.

Donne's vision, even today, seems startlingly contemporary, perhaps ahead of us, too. He felt in his bones the movement toward integration through the painful "contrarieties" of experience. True, he had no experience of the Darwinian, Marxist, Freudian exodus that pushed us through the twentieth century and hurled us into the twenty-first, enabling us to enter into simultaneously the promised land and the wasteland. Yet he anticipated our experience of reality, and our recovering the understanding of the church as that of the exodus, as a nomadic, pilgrim reality. Life was a peregrination and the church, for Donne, was the caravan. The human race thus recapitulates the exodus. The church is on the march from Egypt to Jerusalem.

This exodus has to be subjective and personal, and only then can we proceed to the objective and communal. There is no value in proclaiming a universal gospel unless that gospel be for me. There is no point in promulgating a doctrine of the church as the body of Christ unless I have been engrafted into Christ, who is its head. Thus Donne writes:

As thou hast enlightened and enlarged me to contemplate thy great-
ness, O God, descend thou and stoop down to see my infirmities and
the Egypt in which I live; and (If thy good pleasure be such) hasten
mine Exodus and deliverance, for I desire to be dissolved, and be with
thee.[127]

Provisions for our exodus are to be found in the Scriptures and in the
sacraments, and these are the twin pillars on which the church is founded.
The Bible, as interpreted by the church, gives the direction. It is the compass.
The sacraments, as administered by the church, provide sustenance for the
journey. In the church, individual and collective considerations are beautifully poised, and only in the church is their true balance. Donne's awareness of
himself as primarily a Christian rather than a member of a specific church is
itself an Anglican characteristic.

Donne was a moderate Erasmian Catholic, the *via media* being the *via
regia* between Protestants and Papists. But the most important thing to
remember is that the church is *in via*, on pilgrimage. He wrote, "The Church
is in a warfare, the Church is in a pilgrimage and therefore there is not
setling." There is, he argues, no evidence for the existence of a church that
"must bee Super Catholicke, and Super Universall above all the Churches of
the world. *Ubi libellus?* Where is your evidence? There is no evidence unless
we mistake the superedifications [the bits added]—for foundations: The
peace of the Church, the plenty of the Church, the ceremonies of the Church,
the *sua*, but not *illa*, they are hers but they are not she." What did he mean?
The *sua* are the incidentals. The *illa* are the essentials. Telling the difference
is difficult and elusive, because we are tempted to locate catholicity in the
incidentals; in the ceremonies and polity of the church, and not in the *essentials*, which is Christ and "his inestimable benefits." Repentance, the forgiveness of sins, the death and resurrection of Christ "are that Doctrine which
coagulates and gathers the Church into a body and makes it Catholicke."

All the powers of Donne's intellect were required to maintain the equilib-
rium between the personal and the collective in his understanding of the
church. The church is founded upon that Rock, which is Christ, but it is not
itself the Rock, capable of claiming infallible "locall and personall succession." Any claim to succession in human terms must face the fact of historical interruption and corruption. The catholicity of the Church is a gift and a
peculiarly eschatological one; that is, one that only becomes clear at the Last
Judgment. It should keep us humble and expectant.

Donne would have described his position as "mediocre." Anglicanism,
both Catholic and Reformed, prides itself on its "mediocrity," in the sense in
which he used the word. It is the way of moderation without lukewarmness,
the state of being poised in a middle ground between two extremes. The

Anglican Church, at its best, is mediocre, in the seventeenth-century meaning of the word. At its worst, it is mediocre in the twenty-first-century sense. The word enthusiasm also comes to mind in both its ancient and modern senses: "the severe and unrectified Zeal" of the one and the bracing challenge of the other. The Church of England sought to be unenthusiastic in the former sense at the risk of falling into being unenthusiastic in the latter. Anglicanism is moderate in insisting on the contingent nature of most things ecclesiastical, and in refusing to think of them as necessary. This can be weakness, I admit, for sometimes essentials get lost in the Anglican passion for moderation. It is a matter of indifference to the Anglican, John Donne, that there are several churches with different polities and customs, since there is, in essence, "but one Church, journying to one Hierusalem, and directed by one guide, Christ Jesus."

> In my poor opinion the form of God's worship, established in the Church of England be more convenient and advantageous than of any other Kingdome, both to provide and kindle devotion, and also fix it, that it stray not into infinite expansion and Subdivisions; (into the former of which, Churches utterly despoyl'd of Ceremonies seem to me to have fallen; and the Roman Church, by presenting innumerable objects, into the latter).[128]

Just so Anglicanism, to its adherents, seems to be "more convenient." That is all. That is sufficient. This does not mean one is not an Anglican by conviction, but rather that Anglicanism itself can never be an object of faith. The catholicity of the church is a given that unifies all the contradictions, paradoxes, tensions, and polarities of existence. The church gives Donne's passionate individualism an anchor, a place in which to breathe freely and move about openly. It is not the charnel house of the soul; it is the ground of its existence.

Perhaps Donne's most famous passage concerning the catholicity of the church is in his "Devotions upon Emergent Occasions," written during a period of severe illness and published in 1624. The doctrine of the church emerges from Donne's reflection on his experience, with thought transmuted into feeling: "The Church is Catholicke, universal, so are all her Actions; All that she does, belongs to all. When she baptizes a child, that action concerns mee; for that this child is thereby converted to that Head which is my Head too, and engrafted in that body, whereof I am a member."[129]

Donne's sense of his solidarity with the human race does not, in the end, contradict his sense of uniqueness. Mankind has a common end—death—which unites us all in a common hope. Mankind is all of a piece, and we are united by the tolling of a bell. You will die. Such is our common catholic end.

This basic fact informs Donne's attitude to others, giving impetus to his preaching and fire to his sense of mission. It was Donne who preached the first Anglican missionary sermon to the honourable Company of the Virginian Plantation on November 13, 1622, just thirty-five years after the first English child, Virginia Dare, was baptized in the New World. The alliance between evangelical zeal and commercial venture was, as one would expect, short-lived. Donne had a doubly difficult task in preaching to the merchant adventurers in 1622. Not only had he to outline, for the members of the company, their Christian duty toward the original inhabitants of Virginia, the Indians, but he had to do this in the face of recent news that these very Indians had killed some 350 English settlers that same year.

Earlier that year, on Easter Monday, Donne had proclaimed:

> A Man is thy Neighbour, by his Humanity not by his Divinity; by his Nature, not by his Religion: A Virginian is thy neighbor, as well as a Londoner; and all men are in every good man's Diocese, and Parish.[130]

This was Donne's method. Begin with what is given—that is, what is natural—and build on that. The doctrine of the church is grounded in our common humanity, a fact that the Virginians soon forgot and which most men choose to repress. Donne does not despise commercial enterprise, man's natural desire for position and place, but builds on this brilliantly. He is careful for the prerogatives of King Charles, but more careful for those of the King of kings. He presents to the Honourable Company of the Virginian Plantation an image of the pilgrim church that needs revival today:

> You shall have made this land, which is but as the Suburbs of the old world, a Bridge, a Gallery to the new; to joyne all to that world that shall never grow old, the Kingdome of heaven, You shall add persons to this Kingdome and to the Kingdome of heaven, and add names to the Bookes of our Chronicles, and to the Booke of Life.[131]

Donne, the metaphysical, could live simultaneously in two worlds: in the world of England in 1622, and the world in which human brotherhood and solidarity was a divine gift and imperative. He saw that eschatological dimension, which always anticipates the end, of the church. He lived within that vision and it made and marred him as a man and as a Christian. He poured himself out in the attempt to articulate this vision, to make visible the Christ, to share with others the glorious affliction of transcendence, the affliction that man is driven always to be more.

The church itself is the sacrament of this transcendence; it is the arena in which Christ is made present and visible. It is a meeting place for all the warring elements in Donne's soul, a place of wholeness, of totality, of participation. Christ, for Donne, is the dazzling particular focused on the universal, but not in any easy or naive way, for he was well aware of the tough edges of existence within which divinity was manifest. Transcendence is not "up there," or "outside" but within the fabric of the world, within the labyrinth of the soul. Christ is the reality that both infused his flesh and holds the world in being.

Donne knew this from bitter experience and crushing disappointment. As a young man, he had misunderstood the glorious reality of divinized flesh. The Word became flesh was turned upside down so that the flesh became the Word: an easy but fatal error. Nevertheless, the fleshliness of his poetry is that which, in the end, gives sacramental depth to his theology. Nothing is wasted. He knew that love, to be love, has to be particular, has to be enfleshed. He knew also that love involves the surrendering of the self. He knew that extinction is a prerequisite for resurrection. His creative preoccupation with death is the leitmotif of his thrilling resurrection sermons. In Christ he perceives that sexuality, marvelous as it is, is but the potent symbol of an even more robust love.

Christ, like all human beings, is unfathomable. He cannot be totally understood but he can be touched and embraced. Every human being is a mystery simultaneously palpable and unfathomable. We live the paradox in which every human heart, like the divine essence, is both communicable and incommunicable *at the same time*. Christ is both alchemist and elixir, the maker of the cure and the cure. He is the drinkable gold that transforms our wounded nature and enables us to both live the mystery and begin to see at least some resolution to the apparent contradictions of existence. He transfigures our either/or into both/and.

> He was all gold when he lay downe, but rose
>   All tincture, and doth not alone dispose
> Leaden and iron will to good, but is
> Of power to make even sinfull flesh like his.[132]

This was the miracle of the incarnation: the visibility of the invisible God, in which we are invited to participate. Ours is a journey to the divinizing of our flesh, a movement from darkness to light. The compass for this hazardous adventure is "the essential Word of God, the Son of God, Christ Jesus . . . He was God, humbled in the flesh; he was Man received into glory. . . . Here is the compass of all time, as time was distributed in the Creation, . . . darkness, and then light: the Evening and the Morning made the day."[133]

God not only provides the compass for our journey but also our sustenance along the way: "the visible sacraments," made of palpable and digestible elements—bread and wine and water. It is thus that divinity is

manifested in the fabric of the world, that world that Donne neither under-
stated nor undervalued. It takes time to learn to perceive divinity. It is a hard
school in which particulars are sifted, sorted, and rejected until the particular emerges—the icon of the universal. The Christian is the one who has
graduated from the grammar school of typology—that is, the fascination
with minutiae and with instances, and entered the university of the Logos,
moving from mere examples to the living presence of Christ. Christ is present in and to the stuff of things, if only we could see.

St. Paul, for Donne, was the great example of a transfigured life, a man
transformed by the "real presence of Christ," by the visibility of God.

> Here was a true Transubstantiation, and a new Sacrament. These few
> words, Saul, Saul, why persecutest thou me, are words of a consecra-
> tion; after these words, Saul was no longer Saul, but he was Christ:
> *Vivit in me Christus* [Christ lives in me], says he.[134]

Each human being is called to be the living sacrament of Christ's visibility in the world. To do this we have to be converted. We have to be consecrat-
ed—to be transubstantiated—by a descent into nothingness, because "there
is a good nullification of heart, a good bringing of the heart to nothing." This
nullification, this mortification is the prelude to a new creation:

> When . . . I come to such a melting and pouring out of my heart, that
> there be no spirit, that is, none of mine own spirit left in me; when I
> have so exhausted, so evacuated myself, that is all confidence in myself,
> that I come into the hands of my God, as pliably, as ductily, as that first
> clod of earth, of which he made me in Adam this is a blessed nullifica-
> tion of the heart. When I say to my self I am nothing; and then say to
> God, Lord, though I be nothing, yet behold, I present thee as much as
> thou hadst to make the whole world of; O thou that mad'st the whole
> world of nothing, make me, that am nothing in my own eyes, a new
> Creature in Christ Jesus: This is a blessed nullification, a glorious anni-
> hilation of the heart. So is there also a blessed nullification thereof, in
> the contrition of heart, in the sense of my sins; when, as a sharp winde
> may have worn out a Marble Statue . . . so my holy tears, made holy in
> his Blood that gives them a tincture. . . . have worn out my Marble
> Heart, and emptied the room of that former heart, and so give God a
> Vacuity, a new place to create a heart in.[135]

This is the creative emptiness of the mystic who understands our very
being to be essentially a capacity for God and therefore in need of emptying
in order to be filled. The more we are full of ourselves, the less life there is in

us. Christ came precisely to take our "nothing" and make it "someone." It is this nothing—which we must offer to God in order that he may create us anew out of nothing—that we truly are. God was in Christ to save us from the ultimate absurdity—the emptiness of despair and spiritual exhaustion. The salvation offered in Christ is both free and universal: two facts unpalatable to those who would count God's elect or limit his salvation.

> To save this body from the condemnation of everlasting corruption, where the wormes that we breed are our betters, because they have life, where the dust of dead kings is blowne into the street, and the dust of the street is blowne into the River, and the muddy River tumbled into the Sea, and the Sea remaunded into all the veynes and channels of the earth; to save this body from everlasting dissolution, dispersion, dissipation, and to make it in a glorious Resurrection, not onely a Temple of the holy Ghost, but a Companion of the holy Ghost in the kingdome of heaven, This Christ became this Jesus.[136]

It must have been magnificent to hear these words straight from the preacher's mouth, as Donne proclaimed the incarnation. To reject this free gift, he insisted, either by excluding others or excluding the self, is the deepest folly. One action smacks of tyranny and usurpation, the other of rebellious melancholy.

No one could accuse Donne of not having an adequate and deep sense of sin in general and of his own sin in particular. The question is, which is the greater, man's sin or God's love? To exalt the former at the expense of the latter is disproportionate and a subtle form of pride,

> even in this inordinate dejection thou exaltest thy selfe above God, and makest thy worst better than his best, thy sins larger than his mercy. Christ hath a Greek name, and an Hebrew name; Christ is Greek, Jesus is Hebrew; he had commission to save all nations, and he hath saved all; Thou givest him another name . . . Abaddon, and Apollyn, a Destroyer; when thou wilt not apprehend him as a Saviour, and love him so.[137]

To deny others the grace of God is to block out Christ, to diminish his visibility, to impoverish God. Sin is the masking of the visibility of Christ to the world by his followers. We have, by our darkening sin, "wounded him, and lam'd him by our oppression, we had need provide God an Hospitall."

The relationship between Christ and the believer is very subtle. Nowhere does Donne suggest that God somehow needs our response to maintain the universe. Nor does he suggest that our submission is total annihilation. We are not absorbed into the Godhead but invited to communion. When we sin we grieve God, but we do not hamper him. What amazes Donne is the deference and reticence of God. That God would so pour himself out for us is too wonderful. Thus Donne reflects on the divine self-emptying.

> Remember that our Saviour Christ himselfe, in many actions and passions of our humane nature, and infirmities, smothered that Divinity, and suffered it not to worke, but yet it was always in him, and wrought most powerfully in the deepest danger; when he was absolutely dead, it raised him again Christ slumbred the Godhead in himselfe.[138]

God smothers his divinity in Christ for our sake, letting it slumber in flesh, in the ordinary and the commonplace, in ordinances and sacraments, in bread and wine. We eat and we become what we eat since "the end of all bodily eating is Assimilation . . . that meat may be made idem corpus, the same body that I am; so the end of all spirituall eating is Assimilation too, That after all Hearing, and all Receiving, I may be made idem spiritus cum Domino [one spirit with the Lord]."[139]

Our bodies are the organ in which God breathes. We are body, mind, and Holy Spirit and are human insofar as we have yielded up that total vacuity in which the spirit dwells. The body, as the temple of the Holy Ghost, is made in "consultation of the whole Trinity." The wonder is that God, who is spirit, should have such an affection for this earthly body of ours, although to do so allows his divinity to sleep. The visibility of Christ is not thrust upon us. It is a veiled visibility for the sake of love. Love, after all, is not love when there is force. "Christ saves no man against his will. There is a word crept into the later school, that deludes many a man; they call it Irrestibility . . . Christ beats his Drum, but he does not Press men; Christ is serv'd with Voluntaries."[140]

The life of Christ was a continual kenosis—self-giving. In the light of the seventeenth-century mood, of its religious intolerance, of the forces of the Reformation and Counter-Reformation hardening behind the walls of Geneva and Rome, Donne's theology is all the more remarkable. He preached an open Christ present in all churches, and while he was not afraid to defend his Anglicanism, he knew that it was but the form, the fragile shell of a universal gospel. We may rage and rant, but Christ, the image of the invisible God, quietly and gently accomplishes his purpose.

Donne, preaching at St. Paul's on Christmas Day, 1626, continues the kenosis theme:

> The whole life of Christ was a continuall Passion; others die Martyrs, but Christ was born a Martyr. He found a Golgotha, (where he was

crucified) even in Bethlehem, where he was born; For, to his tender-
nesse then, the strawes were almost as sharp as the thornes after; and
the Manger as uneasie at first, as his Crosse at last. His birth and death
were but one continuall act, and his Christmas day and his Good
Friday, are but the evening and morning of one and the same day.[141]

There is no place better to catch the visibility of Christ in this world than
in the passion of the poor. There the reticence and deference are most manifest since the poor are:

Nuda Imago . . . it is much a harder thing, and there is much more art
showed in making a naked picture, than in all the rich attire that can
be put upon it. And howsoever the rich man, that is invested in Power,
and Greatnesse, may be a better picture of God, of God considered in
himself, who is all Greatnesse, all Power, yet of God considered in
Christ . . . the poor man is the better picture . . . Christ himself carries
this consideration . . . not to a proximity onely but to an identity, The
poore are He . . . He is the poore. And so, he that oppresseth the poore,
reproaches God, God in his Orphans, God in his Image, God in the
Members of his owne Body, God in the Heirs of his Kingdom, God in
himself, in his own person.[142]

God, in the world and especially in the poor, is highly visible. He can be
seen, touched, handled, abused, and betrayed in Christ. There is nothing
made that does not manifest God. A gnat, a worm tell me simply, God is,
because "[t]he whole frame of the world is the Theatre, and every creature
the stage, the medium, the glasse in which we may see God."[143] Donne thinks
that to be a true atheist you would have to pluck out your eyes. Look at a
blade of grass, a leaf, a lump of rock and sense the presence of the Maker.
Nature reveals the presence of God but not the essence—the secret purposes of God. Revelation is needed for us to interpret what we see, and Christ is
the image of the invisible God.

Donne passed onto others his watchful eye and became for them an icon
of the resurrection. Isaak Walton found, in Donne, a lively image of Christ, a
mortal frame that was destined not only to become "a small quantity of
Christian dust," but also to be raised to newness of life.

Salvation, for Donne, was nothing less than the recovery of the
Trinitarian life in true Augustinian fashion; the recovery of memory, understanding, and will. All three he abandoned to God. What is impressive is that
for Donne each yielding, each giving up is not a rejection but a transfiguration. Sexuality is not repressed but transcended. Ambition is not denied but
redirected. Reason is never incarcerated but truly liberated by knowledge of

its limitations. All are perceived as gift, as grace, as gospel. Donne's transfiguration was long, painful, and glorious. Its incubation period was the nine years of testing (1601–1610); its fruition in this life, his magnificent funeral sermon "Death's Duell" on the first Friday in Lent, 1631. Donne was ready for death. He knew that

> [m]any graines make up the bread that feeds us; and many thornes make up the Crowne that must glorifie us . . . But . . . since that Crown is made of thorns, be not without them when you contemplate Christ. . . . Find thorns within; a wounding sense of sin, bring you the thorns, and Christ will make it a crown.[144]

Donne's crown of thorns finally began to form in the fall of 1630, the occasion of his last illness, when he was so ill that he could not preach the "Gunpowder Plot Sermon" on November 5. A dying man, he eventually climbed into the pulpit of St. Paul's at the beginning of Lent, 1631. In the presence of the king, the dean preached on the death of God:

> That God . . . the Lord of life could dye, is a strange contemplation; That the red Sea could bee drie . . . is strange . . . but supermiraculous that God could dye; but that God would dye is an exaltation of that. . . . There was nothing more free, more voluntary, more spontaneous than the death of Christ. . . . There wee leave you in that blessed dependency, to hang upon him that hangs upon the Crosse, there bathe in his teares, there suck at his wounds, and lye downe in peace in his grave, till hee vouchsafe you a resurrection, and an ascension into that Kingdome, which hee hath purchased for you, with the inestimable price of his incorruptible blood.[145]

Izaak Walton writes that Donne preached this sermon "as if having done this, there remained nothing for him to doe, but to die." The visibility of Christ in a man prepared to die, the final affliction where the longing for transcendence becomes a reality in the life to come: all this was present in the dying of John Donne.

The Anglican Pilgrimage Today

John Donne and people like him make me proud to be an Anglican and Anglicanism has an important vocation in the family of the church today. At our best, we not only tolerate but celebrate difference. Rabbi Jonathan Sacks asks, "Why, if God is the God of all humanity, is there not one faith, one truth?"[146] He suggests that God calls each of us to be unique, and all of us to rejoice in the dignity of difference.

As the great rabbis observed some eighteen hundred years ago, when a human being makes many coins in the same mint, they all come out the same. God makes every human being in the same mint, in the same image, his own, and yet we all come out differently. The religious challenge is to find God's image in someone who is not in our image, in someone whose color is different, whose culture is different, who speaks a different language, tells a different story, and worships God in a different way. *This is a paradigm shift in understanding monotheism.*

A great contemporary Anglican, Phyllis Tickle, in her book *Prayer Is a Place: America's Religious Landscape Observed*, writes, "Religion is messy and it is highly flammable." Indeed, her own messy spiritual pilgrimage, she says, has been a movement from the "one way only" dogma of her upbringing to "the mercy of God and many manifestations" position, "primarily because the New Testament seems to me not only to leave that door wide open, but also to point earnestly in that direction." She is confident of universal salvation for all, with "[m]ercy over justice. No questions asked or even raised." This generosity of spirit is at the heart of Anglican orthodoxy—right believing for Anglicans.[147]

Here's a rabbinic story: When God was about to create Adam, the ministering angels split into contending groups. Some were in favor of Adam being created; others were against it—and that's why, the story goes, Psalm 85, verse 11, proclaims, "Mercy and truth collided, righteousness and peace clashed." Rabbi Jonathan Sacks points to a bold rabbinic interpretation. "God takes truth and throws it to the ground, meaning: for life to be livable, truth on earth cannot be what it is in heaven." May God rescue us from the ideologues and the fundamentalists—the people of faith with bombs in their shoes.

The poet W. H. Auden wrote:

> The Catholic faith . . . while it condemns no temperament as incapable of salvation, flatters none as being in less peril than any other. In the same way [a Christian] has to make his public confession in a church which is not confined to his sort, to those with whom by nature he feels at home, for in it there is neither Jew nor German, East nor West, boy nor girl, smart nor dumb, boss nor worker, Bohemian nor bourgeois, no elite of any kind; indeed there are not even Christians there, for Christianity is a way, not a state, and a Christian is never something one is, only something one can pray to become.[148]

And James Carroll asks,

> What if . . . human beings are never in full possession of the truth, but must constantly seek it in new experience in a dialogue of respect and

mutuality with others? Does this equal relativism? No, for the absolute does exist . . . but it exists not as turf to be defended, nor as proof of one's own superiority, but as the horizon toward which one is forever on pilgrimage. Instead of seeing human beings as creatures who are already fully defined, and whose moral obligations are therefore already fully promulgated, the "pilgrim" knows that human meaning and morality are still unfolding.[149]

What if we are on pilgrimage? What if there are not even Christians in church yet, for Christianity is a way, not a state, and a Christian is never something one is, only something one can pray to become? What if, instead of seeing human beings as creatures who are already fully defined, and whose moral obligations are therefore already fully promulgated, the "pilgrim" sees that human meaning and morality are still unfolding? What if the Anglican communion has yet to come into its own? What if the best is yet to come? What if . . . we started treating one another in such a way that the world would look at us and say, "See, how those Christians love one another!"

Afterword

I wonder how much our faith has to do with spirit and attitude? For example, the Anglican approach to orthodoxy, particularly with regard to Mary, became very clear to me one summer on vacation in Tuscany. Attending the Feast of the Assumption in the little community of Caiano was like seeing dogma in action. It was folk religion at its best, without the cold touch of the legal mind to render it literal and technical. The people knew they had a woman in heaven on their side and that she was forever pointing to her Son.

It was an evening mass outside in the field by the church. At the elevation of the host, the large sow, her feet up on top of the wall, squealed in excitement, the chickens were riled, and many at the back of the crowd shushed four noisy women who were making a racket talking too loudly. Yet the sacred moment was neither marred nor compromised. The church was at its best, a sign to the world that there was much more to the world than the world could possibly imagine. The priest had preached on the Magnificat and about Mary being a sign of how much God loves us. There she is—humble and always presenting her Son to the world—in heaven, still caring for us.

The whole scheme of redemption depended on her obedience. Because of her, we are well-connected. We have a home. We have a place to go. And we can live in hope because we are deeply loved. Now, while there is, of course, more to be said about the dogma of the assumption than this, the church in the sacrament on this feast day communicated to the congregation the essential message of the work of salvation.

They went home that night praising the Madonna and knowing that they were in good hands, and that in spite of all the tragedy and pain in the world, the forces of darkness didn't have the last word. There weren't any systematic theologians present, but that evening the church did what it does at its best: allows the dogmas of the church to speak through the action of the sacrament and, because of this, people live and die in hope.

The mass began a little after six-thirty in a field just by the church of Santa Maria. Mary was all ready for the procession—set up in the little medieval church with flowers and a halo of electric lights. Preparations had begun that morning; and the day before, after the regular mass, my wife and I volunteered to help with the next day's preparation. The sky that morning wasn't very promising—unusual for August. We'd had violent thunderstorms and even one with great lumps of hail. There were threatening black clouds but also bright sun shining through them that morning.

What were we, two stray Anglicans, to make of it all? We were warmly welcomed and were fully embraced by this grassroots Catholicism—summed up in a little statement in a pamphlet in the church in the next town: *Dio è Comunione di Amore* [God Is Communion of Love]. At the heart of our shared faith is this simple Trinitarian statement. Here was the church being the church: "And they continued steadfastly in the apostles' teaching, in the fellowship, in the breaking of bread and in the prayers" (Acts 2:42 RSV). There were the devout, the casual, the unbelievers even, and those two almost but not quite Roman Catholics—all of us at the feast, no one turned away. *The Catechism for Adults* says this concerning the Eucharist—which nourishes our communion with God and with one another—"Mystery of Love! Symbol of Unity! Bond of Charity." We saw all three that night. We saw and experienced the "dogma" of the God who is communion-in-love. We should never forget what God is doing in spite of our misunderstandings and divisions. God reigns in spite of our fear of the divine generosity. That night we experienced a taste of heaven.

Archbishop Peter Carnley tells a story of an imam and a fundamentalist. The imam was speaking at an English cathedral and the fundamentalist was outraged. "What do you think you are doing? Why are you here?" The dean invited the imam to respond. "I'm here because I love Jesus. Do you?" Why are we here? What are we about? Loving Jesus might not be all there is to the Christian faith, but it's a start.

AS YOU, FATHER, ARE IN ME AND I AM IN YOU,
MAY THEY ALSO BE IN US, SO THAT THE WORLD
MAY BELIEVE THAT YOU HAVE SENT ME. (JOHN 17:21)

NOTES

Foreword

1. See for example, George Sumner's essay "After Dromatine" in *The Anglican Theological Review* (cited hereafter as *ATR*) 87, no. 4 (2005) (a volume dedicated to responses to the Windsor Report), 561.

2. Ibid., 563.

3. See my doctoral thesis, *Herbert Hamilton Kelly: A Study in Failure—A Contribution to the Search for a Credible Catholicism*, University of Nottingham, 1971.

4. Ian T. Douglas, "Authority, Unity, and Mission in the Windsor Report," in *ATR* 87, no. 4 (2005), 573.

5. See Scott Cowdell's "On Loving the Church," www.stpaulsmanuka.org.au/Loving%20the%20Church.htm.

6. See the editorial in *The Tablet*, July 9, 2005, 2.

7. *Gaudium et Spes* (36), quoted by Nicholas Boyle in *The Tablet*, July 9, 2005, 12.

8. Kennedy Frasers, in an article on the Church of England in *The New Yorker*, December 4, 1995, 48ff.

9. *The Tablet*, July 9, 2005, 2.

10. Julie Irwin, "Cardinal Bernardin Was a Leader," *Cincinnati Enquirer*, November 14, 1996.

11. Clifford Longley in *The Tablet*, May 29, 1999, 734.

12. Peter Cornwell, *The Tablet*, July 19, 2003.

13. See, for example, Bernard McGinn's *The Growth of Mysticism: Gregory the Great through the 12th Century*, Volume II of *The Presence of God: A History of Western Christian Mysticism* (New York: Crossroad, 1994), 94 ff.

14. See Henry Chadwick's "History of the Oxford Movement 150 Years On" in *Lift High the Cross: The Oxford Movement Sesquicentennial* (cited hereafter as *Lift High the Cross*), ed. J. Robert Wright (Cincinnati: Forward Movement, 1984), 69–71.

Part I: Fundamentalism and Scientism:
A Plague on Both Their Houses

15. John le Carré, *Absolute Friends* (New York: Little Brown, 2004), 419–20.

16. See Paul Smith's review, "Good Losers," of A. N. Wilson's *After the Victorians, 1901–1953* (London: Hutchinson, 2005), in *The Times Literary Supplement* (hereafter cited as *TLS*), October 14, 2005, 6.

17. Ian McEwan, *Enduring Love* (New York: Random House, 1997), 36.

18. Ibid., 53.

19. Ibid., 74–75.

20. Ibid., 145.

21. Ibid., 158.

22. Ibid., 161–162.

23. Ibid., 196.

24. Ian McEwan, *Saturday* (New York: Doubleday, 2005) 17.

25. See Jonathan Luxmore and Jolanta Babiuch, "Deicide in North Oxford," in *The Tablet*, Christmas 2002, pp. 9ff.

26. See Stéphane Courtois and Rémi Kauffer, *Le Livre Noir de Communism: Crimes, Terreur, Rèpression* (Paris: Robert Laffont, 1997).

27. Quoted by Rollo May, *The Cry for Myth* (New York: W. W. Norton, 1991), 63.

28. Jonathan Sacks, *The Dignity of Difference: How to Avoid the Clash of Civilizations* (London and New York: Continuum International Publishing Group, 2002), 46.

29. Timothy Radcliffe, O.P., *Seven Last Words* (London and New York: Burns & Oates, 2004), 85.

30. Ibid., 93.

31. Peter Carnley, *Reflections in Glass: Trends and Tensions in the Contemporary Anglican Church* (New York: HarperCollins, 2004), 20.

32. Michael Lind in the *Wilson Quarterly* (Winter 2000).

33. Rowan Williams, *Open to Judgment: Sermons and Addresses* (London: DLT, 1994), 35.

34. Edmund Campion's review, "Gospel Imperialism," of Chris McGillion's *The Chosen Ones: The Politics of Salvation in the Anglican Church* in the *TLS*, November 4, 2005, 29.

35. Carnley, *Reflections in Glass*, 15.

36. Ibid., 15–16.

37. See ibid., quoted by Carnley.

38. Review by David Howell of *This Will Hurt*, ed. Digby Anderson (London: Social Affairs Unit, 1995) in *TLS*, September 22, 1995. The last section is a quotation from Michael Aeschliman's essay.

39. John Henry Newman, *The Development of Christian Doctrine* (Bloomington, IN: University of Notre Dame Press, 1989), 41.

40. See Stephen Bates, "Is the End Nigh?" in *The Tablet*, June 25, 2005, 14.

41. Rowan Williams, *Open to Judgment*, 35.

42. On a card sent from *poetrymagazine.org*, November 2005.

43. Nigel Williams, *Witchcraft* (London: Farber & Farber, 1987), 52.

44. Ellen T. Charry's editorial in *Theology Today*, January 2001, 453.

45. Quoted in the *Chronicle of Higher Education*, June 23, 2000; see also John Millbank, *The Word Made Strange: Theology, Language, Culture* (Oxford: Blackwell, 1997).

46. Huston Smith, *The Soul of Christianity* (HarperSanFrancisco, 2005), xviii.

47. Ibid., 25.

48. Ibid., quoted by Smith, 58; Stephen Dunn, *Selected Poems 1974–1994* (New York: W. W. Norton, 1995), 183.

49. Ibid., 211.

50. Ibid.

51. Michael Arditti, *Easter* (London: Arcadia Books, 2000), 77–78.

52. Ibid., 80.

53. Ibid., 377.

54. John W. Gardner, "Building Community" (Washington, D.C.: Independent Sector, 1991), 15.

55. Rowan Williams, *A Ray of Darkness* (Cambridge, MA: Cowley, 1995), 88.

56. Ibid.

57. *Newsweek*, May 23, 2005.

58. Williams, *A Ray of Darkness*, 90.

59. Ibid.

60. Lewis Lapham, *Harper's Magazine*, October 2005.

61. *Harper's Magazine*, November 2005.

Part II: The Anglican Conversation:
Caricatures of Anglicanism and Its Discontents

62. John Patrick Shanley, *Doubt* (New York: Theatre Communication Group, 2005), vii.

63. Richard Holloway, "Social and Political Implications of the Oxford Movement," in *Lift High the Cross*, 30–31.

64. Ibid., 45. The reference to John Keble is in one of Pusey's letters written in his old age: "What a picture it gives one to see dear Keble finding his way with a lantern through the snow to his little church at 5:30 on a winter morning to say the Litany for the Church 'in its present distress'" (see 33).

65. Just try "Googling" something like "The Anglican Genius" on the Internet.

66. Paul G. Kuntz, "Whitehead the Anglican and Russell the Puritan: The Traditional Origins of Muddleheadedness and Simplemindedness," *Process Studies* 17, no. 1, (1988), 43.

67. Matthew Parris, "Why the Church of England Is Our Best Defense against Religious Enthusiasm," *The Spectator*, April 2, 2005.

68. Walker Percy, *The Second Coming* (New York: Farrar, Straus & Giroux, 1980), 190.

69. Peter Brook, *The Empty Space* (London: Penguin, 1968), 50–51.

70. Kennedy Fraser, *The New Yorker*, December 4, 1995, 48ff.

71. Ibid.

72. Don Cupitt, *After God: The Future of Religion* (New York: Harper Collins/Basic Books, 1997), 74.

73. Alasdair McIntyre, *After Virtue* (Notre Dame, IN: University of Notre Dame Press, 1982).

74. Peter L. Berger, *A Far Glory: The Quest for Faith in an Age of Credulity* (New York: Free Press, 1992).

75. Thomas Cahill, *How the Irish Saved Civilization* (New York: Doubleday/Anchor Books, 1995), 217–18.

76. Rowan Williams, *On Christian Theology* (Oxford: Blackwell, 2000).

77. Rowan Williams, "On Being Creatures," *On Christian Theology*, 63.

78. Rowan Williams,"The Unity of Christian Truth," *On Christian Theology*, 17.

79. Ibid.

80. Philip Turner, "An Unworkable Theology," *First Things*, June/July 2005, 10ff.

81. Ibid., 10–11.

82. Ibid., 11.

83. Rowan Williams, university sermon, Oxford, November 1981.

Part III: The Promise of Anglican Orthodoxy

84. Timothy Radcliffe, O.P., *I Call You Friends* (London and New York: Continuum, 2001), 52.

85. Bede Griffiths, *The Golden String* (London: Collins, Fontana, 1954).

86. William Johnston, *Arise My Love: Mysticism for a New Era* (Maryknoll, NY: Orbis Books, 2000).

87. For more information, see *Monastic Interreligious Dialogue*, www.monasticdialog.com, sponsored by North American Benedictine and Cistercian Monasteries of Men and Women, especially articles by Father Laurence Freeman, O.S.B., on his meetings with Father Griffiths.

88. Isabel Colegate, *The Summer of the Royal Visit* (New York: Knopf, 1992).

89. Carnley, *Reflections in Glass*, 57.

90. Paul Zahl, "Thoughts on the Windsor Report," *ATR* 87, no. 4 (2005), 580.

91. This section owes a great deal to church historian Eamon Duffy.

92. Eamon Duffy, *Faith of Our Fathers* (New York: Continuum, 2004), 172.

93. Ian McEwan, *Saturday*, 35.

94. See *Encylopaedia of Religion and Ethics*, ed. James Hastings (London: T & T Clark International, 1999).

95. From Sam Keen's unpublished manuscript, tentatively titled *Minor Epiphanies: Confessions of an Agnostic Christian*.

96. Carnley, *Reflections in Glass*, 84

97. Ibid., 25.

98. Ibid.

99. Ibid., 287.

100. Ibid., 48.

101. Quoted by Henri de Lubac, *The Mystery of the Supernatural* (London: Geoffrey Chapman, 1967), 218–19; see also John Meyendorff, *Gregory Palamas: The Triads* (New York: Paulist Press, 1982).

102. Henri de Lubac, *The Mystery of the Supernatural*, 147.

103. Ibid., 219.

104. See Alan Jones, "The Visibility of Christ and the Affliction of Transcendence," *Spirit and Light: Essays in Historical Theory* (New York: Seabury Press, 1976).

105. John Henry Newman, Tract 73: "On the Introduction of Rationalistic Principles to Revealed Religion."

106. Quoted by Carnley, *Reflections in Glass*, 147.

107. Carnley, *Reflections in Glass*, 48. This section owes a great deal to Archbishop Carnley's exposition.

108. *Adversus Eunomius*, 12.

109. Carnley, *Reflections in Glass*, 105.

110. Ibid., 50.

Part IV: Anglicanism's Future? The Clue Is in Our Past

111. See Jacques Barzun, *From Dawn to Decadence* (New York: HarperCollins, 2000), 581–82.

112. See A. M. Allchin's preface in *George Herbert: The Country Parson, The Temple*, ed. John N. Wall (New York: Paulist Press, 1981), xii; Allchin, writing about George Herbert and his contemporaries, outlines some of the characteristics. Also see T. S. Eliot's *For Lancelot Andrewes* (London: Faber & Gwyer, 1928), 17–18.

113. See A. M. Allchin's Preface in *George Herbert*, ix; see also A. M. Allchin's *Participation in God: A Forgotten Strand in Anglican Tradition* (London: DLT, 1988) and other works.

114. Esther de Waal, *The Celtic Way of Prayer* (New York: Doubleday/Image Books, 1996), introduction.

115. Ibid.

116. You will find this and the following extracts in Frederick Quinn's excellent *To Be A Pilgrim: The Anglican Ethos in History* (New York: Crossroad, 2001).

117. Michael Ramsey, *The Gospel and the Catholic Church* (1938; reprint, London: Longmans, 1959), 220.

118. Gerard Manley Hopkins expression.

119. For detailed references, see my essay "The Visibility of Christ and the Affliction of Transcendence" in *Spirit and Light: Essays in Honor of Canon Edward Nason West* (New York: Seabury, 1976).

120. John Donne, *The Sermons of John Donne*, vol. 7, ed. G. R. Potter and Evelyn M. Simpson (Berkeley, CA: University of California Press, 1953–1962), 78.

121. Ibid.

122. Ibid., vol. 8, 332–33.

123. Ibid., vol. 5, 38.

124. Ibid, vol. 9, 166.

125. Ibid., 170–72.

126. Ibid., vol. 4, 301.

127. Evelyn M. Simpson, ed., *Essayes in Divinity* (Oxford: Oxford University Press, 1952), 96.

128. John Donne, "Essays in Divinity" in *Selected Prose*, ed. Helen Garmer and Timothy Healy (Oxford: Oxford University Press, 1967), 77.

129. John Donne, "Devotions Upon Emergent Occasions," in ibid., 51.

130. Donne, *Sermons*, vol. 4, 110.

131. Ibid., 280–81.

132. R. E. Hughes, *The Progress of the Soul: The Interior Career of John Donne* (New York: William Morrow, 1968), 170.

133. Donne, *Sermons*, vol. 3, 302–3.

134. Ibid., vol. 6, 209.

135. Ibid., vol. 9, 177.

136. Ibid., vol. 3, 302–3.

137. Ibid.

138. Ibid., vol. 6, 1 74.

139. Ibid., 223.

140. Ibid., vol. 7, 158.

141. Ibid., 279.

142. Ibid., vol. 8, 285.

143. Ibid., 279.

144. John Donne, letter in *Essays in Celebration*, ed. A. J. Smith (London: Metheun, 1972), 438.

145. Donne, *Sermons*, vol. 10, 229–48.

146. Jonathan Sacks, *The Dignity of Difference: Avoiding the Clash of Civilizations* (New York and London: Continuum International Publishing Group, 2002).

147. Phyllis Tickle, *Prayer Is a Place: America's Religious Landscape Observed* (New York: Doubleday/Random House, 2005), 86.

148. See Adam Gopnik in the *New Yorker*, September 23, 2002, on the poetry of belief—quoting Auden (summarizing his essays and poetry under the heading "How to Love All Mankind While Politely Keeping It Out of Your Garden."

149. James Carroll, *The Boston Globe*.